TOP **10**
PUERTO RICO

CHRISTOPHER P BAKER

EYEWITNESS TRAVEL

Left **Old San Juan** Center **Bacardi Rum's logo** Right **Parque Ceremonial Indígena Caguana**

LONDON, NEW YORK,
MELBOURNE, MUNICH AND DELHI
www.dk.com

Contents

Design, Editorial, and Picture Research by
Quadrum Solutions, Krishnamai, 33B, Sir
Pochkanwala Road, Worli, Mumbai, India

Printed and bound in China by
Leo Paper Products Ltd

First American Edition, 2009
13 14 15 16 10 9 8 7 6 5 4 3 2 1

Published in the United States by
DK Publishing, 375 Hudson Street,
New York, New York 10014

Reprinted with revisions 2011, 2013

Published in the UK by Dorling Kindersley Limited.

A catalog record for this book is available from
the Library of Congress.

ISSN 1479-344X

ISBN 978 0 7566 9682 5

MIX
Paper from
responsible sources
FSC™ C018179
www.fsc.org

Puerto Rico's Top 10

The information in this DK Eyewitness Top 10 Travel Guide is checked regularly.

Every effort has been made to ensure that this book is as up-to-date as possible at the time of
going to press. Some details, however, such as telephone numbers, opening hours, prices,
gallery hanging arrangements and travel information are liable to change. The publishers
cannot accept responsibility for any consequences arising from the use of this book, nor for
any material on third party websites, and cannot guarantee that any website address in this
book will be a suitable source of travel information. We value the views and suggestions of
our readers very highly. Please write to: Publisher, DK Eyewitness Travel Guides,
Dorling Kindersley, 80 Strand, London WC2R 0RL, or email: travelguides@dk.com.

Left **Arecibo Observatory** Center **Museo Indígena Cemí** Right **Castillo de San Cristóbal's entrance**

Left **Scenic Playa Flamenco** Right *Vejigantes,* **Carnaval Ponceño**

PUERTO RICO'S TOP 10

PUERTO RICO'S TOP 10

🔟 Puerto Rico's Highlights

Puerto Rico packs tremendous diversity into a relatively small space. From exquisite coral reefs and white-sand beaches to lush rain forests, desert-dry coastal plains, and a rugged mountain spine, this isle enraptures with physical beauty. Past and present intertwine too, as pre-Columbian sites, massive castles, and charming colonial buildings contrast with hip restaurants, hotels, and nightclubs. Spanish-speaking yet inarguably American in style, the people are equally diverse, reflecting a potpourri of bloodlines – indigenous, African, and European – and a creativity expressed in colorful culture and arts.

1 Old San Juan
This blue-cobbled historic district of restored colonial buildings is the jewel in the capital city's crown. Its delightful plazas, centuries-old cathedrals, and dramatic castles are well-preserved reminders of a bygone era (see pp8–9).

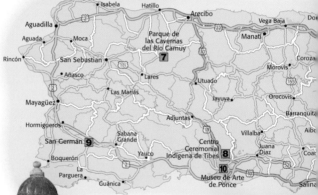

3 Condado
San Juan's lively beach-front is lined with trendy cafés and restaurants, fashionable boutiques, and high-rise hotels interspersed with parks (see pp12–13).

2 Castillo de San Cristóbal
This fortress, which has been restored to its former grandeur, has bulwarks looming over the shoreline, cannons, and other interesting exhibits (see pp10–11).

4 El Yunque
The only tropical rain forest within US territory offers great hiking along mountain trails. Waterfalls and coquí frogs are among the many lures of this natural paradise (see pp14–15).

 Preceding pages **Fortaleza San Felipe del Morro, Old San Juan**

Vieques

This island, off the east coast of Puerto Rico's main island, is surrounded by idyllic beaches. It has become a magnet for independent travelers seeking a laid-back lifestyle and trendy boutique hotels *(see pp16–17)*.

Culebra

Boasting the most spectacular beach in Puerto Rico, this small island is popular with day-trippers and is easily reached by ferry. It also delights snorkelers and surfers *(see pp18–19)*.

Parque de las Cavernas del Río Camuy

Only an hour's drive from the capital, the world's third-largest known cavern system is accessible through guided tours. Floodlights illuminate the dripstone formations *(see pp20–2)*.

Map showing locations:

San Juan — Castillo de San Cristóbal, Condado, Carolina, Loíza, Río Grande, Luquillo, Fajardo, Cayo Lobos, Culebra, El Yunque, Ceiba, Guaynabo, Trujillo Alto, Gurabo, Caguas, San Lorenzo, Las Piedras, Humacao, Isabel Segunda, Vieques, Cayey, Palmas del Mar, Maunabo, Guayama, Sonda de Vieques, Pasaje de Vieques

15 ⌐———— miles ⌐ 0 ⌐ km ————⌐ 15

Museo de Arte de Ponce

This world-class museum displays artworks from the 14th to the 20th centuries, including works by Rossetti, Constable, and Reynolds *(see pp26–7)*.

San Germán

The best-preserved colonial town outside Old San Juan retains its yesteryear mood. Historic buildings here include Puerto Rico's oldest church, which is full of interesting religious antiquities *(see pp24–5)*.

Centro Ceremonial Indígena de Tibes

This pre-Columbian ceremonial site displays well-preserved *bateyes* (ball courts) and sacred petroglyphs. It is the perfect place to learn about ancient Taíno culture *(see pp22–3)*.

🔟 Old San Juan

Old San Juan (Viejo San Juan) is the historic heart of Puerto Rico's capital city. This intimate quarter boasts an astonishing wealth of well-preserved forts, cathedrals, and convents, as well as colorful mansions and other important buildings spanning five centuries. The footsteps of friars and conquistadores seem to echo down cobbled streets and plazas that exude plenty of colonial charm. Easily walkable, the narrow, shaded streets of Old San Juan are lined with museums, hotels, restaurants, boutiques, and trendy bars. No museum piece, this lively quarter is a thriving community where families gather to enjoy the irresistible ambience.

Statue of an immigrant at Plaza del Inmigrante

🎫 Shorts are fine for exploring the old city, but should not be worn in churches or upscale restaurants. Women should cover their shoulders and dress modestly when entering churches.

🍽 The El Patio de Sam *(see p64)* is ideal for a cool drink, snack, or simple meal.

• Casa Blanca: Map T5; Calle San Sebastián 1; 787 725 1454; open 8:30am–4:30pm Wed–Sun
• Fortaleza San Felipe del Morro: Map S4; Calle del Morro; 787 729 6777; open 9am–6pm; adm $3
• Catedral de San Juan Baútista: Map U6; Plazuela de la Monjas
• Instituto de Cultura Puertorriqueña: Map T5; Calle del Morro; 787 724 0700; open 8am–noon & 1–4:30pm Mon–Fri; www.icp.gobierno.pr

Top 10 Features

1 Casa Blanca
2 Fortaleza San Felipe del Morro
3 Castillo de San Cristóbal
4 Plaza de San José
5 Plaza del Inmigrante
6 Paseo de la Princesa
7 Catedral de San Juan Baútista
8 Plaza de Armas
9 Parque de las Palomas
10 Instituto de Cultura Puertorriqueña

Casa Blanca
Considered the oldest continually occupied structure in the western hemisphere, Casa Blanca (1521) *(below)* was built for Ponce de León *(see p30)*. It now houses a museum.

Castillo de San Cristóbal
This massive fortress, built between 1634 and 1783, features seven convoluted lines of defence connected by moats and tunnels *(right)*. It contains cannons as well as an interesting museum *(see pp10–11)*.

Fortaleza San Felipe del Morro
This fortress *(main image)* guards the entrance to San Juan's harbor and took over 200 years to complete. Its stone ramparts rise six levels, and feature cannons that point out to sea. A museum displays military uniforms and weaponry.

Plaza de San José
4 This delightful square is dominated by a bronze statue of Ponce de León *(left)*. The square's restaurants, bars, and cafés come to life at night and are great for people-watching.

Plaza del Inmigrante
5 A wide square by the port, Plaza del Inmigrante features stunning Art Deco and Neo-Classical buildings, and a bust that commemorates all those who came to start life anew in Puerto Rico.

Paseo de la Princesa
6 This promenade *(below)* runs west from Plaza del Inmigrante. The Raíces Fountain at its far western end celebrates the island's indigenous, African, and Spanish heritage.

Catedral de San Juan Baútista
7 The cathedral, completed in 1852 with a part-Neo-Classical, part-Baroque facade and restored in 1917, houses the tomb of Ponce de León. It has a beautiful parquet floor and a trompe l'oeil ceiling.

Plaza de Armas
8 A former parade ground, this leafy plaza is the city's most lively social gathering place by day. It has four statues *(right)* representing the four seasons, and is surrounded by elegant buildings.

Parque de las Palomas
9 Named for the pigeons that flock here, this park atop the city walls is home to Capilla del Cristo – a chapel with an altar that is adorned with silver *milagros* (offerings left in gratitude for favors granted by saints).

Instituto de Cultura Puertorriqueña
10 Housed in a grandiose Neo-Classical building, the institute has a magnificent museum and art gallery featuring exhibits from pre-Columbian times through the colonial and post-colonial periods.

Blue Cobblestones

Old San Juan is paved with oblong cobblestones that were brought over as ballast in Spanish galleons. Cast from furnace slag, they are tinted blue, unlike the gray- and red-tinted cobbles of English-speaking Caribbean islands. Although many streets have been paved over since, restoration has revealed the original cobbles anew.

For more on Puerto Rico's history **See pp30–31.**

Castillo de San Cristóbal

This enormous clifftop fortress, built in stages between 1634 and 1783, covers 27 acres (11 ha) and is one of the largest Spanish castles built in the Americas. Towering 150 ft (45 m) above the Atlantic, this wonderfully preserved marvel of military engineering was connected to Fortaleza San Felipe del Morro (see p8) by bastions stretching along more than half-a-mile (1 km) of shore. Following the Spanish-American War (see p31), this fortress was occupied by the US Army until 1961. Now a UNESCO World Heritage Site, it is managed by the US National Parks Service, whose rangers lead free tours.

The interior of the fort's officers' quarters

Watch for interesting re-enactments in period uniforms, such as the British invasion of 1797, by The Fixed Regiment of Puerto Rico living history group.

Yeyo's, a 10- to 15-minute walk from the fortress, at Calle San Francisco 353 (787 725 9362), is a tiny working-class restaurant serving tasty *criolla* dishes, such as *mofongo (see p50)*, at bargain prices.

- Map W5–X5
- Calle Norzagaray
- 787 729 6960
- Open 9am–6pm
- Adm $5 for both Fortaleza San Felipe del Mono and Castillo de San Cristobal; free for under-15s
- www.nps.gov/saju

Top 10 Features

1. Entrance Gate
2. Plaza de Armas
3. Devil's Sentry Box
4. North Battery
5. Chapel
6. Main Battery
7. Barracks
8. Ordoñez Cannon
9. Great Moat
10. Tunnels

1 Entrance Gate
Approached via a long, sloping ramp that curves through almost 90 degrees, the arched entrance gate *(below)* dates from 1783 and is topped by a decorative cornice with twin globes.

2 Plaza de Armas
The fortress's parade ground was completed in 1783. It is lined with load-bearing casements which were used as barracks, powder magazines, and officers' quarters fronted by a loggia (columned balcony).

3 Devil's Sentry Box
The lonesome Garita del Diablo *(right)*, built in 1634, overhangs the ocean at the tip of the triangular Fuerte del Espigón (Fort of the Point). Guards were stationed here to keep watch for approaching enemy intruders.

4 North Battery

This battery took its present form in the 1890s, when gun emplacements were added in preparation for the Spanish-American War. The officers' quarters were added later

5 Chapel

The simple Capilla de Santa Bárbara, on the west side of Plaza de Armas, is dedicated to Santa Barbara *(left)*, the patron saint of artillerymen, to whom troops prayed for their safe-keeping.

6 Main Battery

This battery is the highest of seven lines of defence intended to protect the city from a land invasion. In 1797, its cannons *(below)* were instrumental in repelling a British invasion led by Sir Ralph Abercrombie.

7 Barracks

The barracks, on the east side of Plaza de Armas, were built atop five massive cisterns. Even today, the soldiers' uniforms hang in the rooms, just as they did in the 18th century.

8 Ordoñez Cannon

This artillery piece, developed by Spanish Captain Salvador Díaz Ordoñez, fired the opening shots of the Spanish-American War on May 12, 1898, against the USS *Yale*.

9 Great Moat

The 16-ft (5-m) thick walls rise over a wide moat intended to slow the advance of invaders and expose them to deadly fire from the sentry boxes above.

10 Tunnels

An extensive tunnel system *(right)* connected the center of the fort to the defensive elements and allowed protected movement of troops and artillery. The tunnels were mined and could be detonated to deny the enemy access.

Haunted Sentry Box

Puerto Rican legend has it that the Devil's Sentry Box is named for a sentry who was snatched by the devil, and left behind only his musket and uniform. The truth seems to be that the soldier craftily abandoned his post for his loved one, but many locals still believe that the *garita* is haunted.

TOP 10 Condado

The fast-moving metropolis of San Juan is at its most glamorous in Condado, a beachfront zone that extends east from the old town along miles of shorefront lined with condominiums, hotels, and casinos. Condado melds into two other beach neighborhoods, Ocean Park and Isla Verde, forming an upscale residential district. This bustling area, which occupies a slender isthmus wedged between the Atlantic Ocean and Laguna del Condado, teems with Art Deco and modernist structures. This is the place to be on weekends when the young and young-at-heart flock to sun themselves by day and to party by night.

Avenida Ashford

⚡ Be cautious where you swim. Many parts of the beaches are rocky, and some areas have dangerous undertows. Ask your hotel concierge for local conditions.

🍹 When you want to splurge, dine at Zest *(see p65)* – try the signature Sandgria or Oceanberry cocktails.

• Map W1–X1

Top 10 Features

1. Beaches
2. Avenida Ashford
3. Watersports
4. Laguna del Condado
5. Juan Bobo Statue
6. La Ventana al Mar
7. Art Deco Architecture
8. Fine Restaurants
9. Ocean Park
10. Casinos

Beaches
1 Unfurling along more than 5 miles (8 km) of shorefront, the talcum-white beaches of Condado draw locals on weekends to sunbathe, kite-surf, and mingle beneath the palms *(above)*. Most of the beaches have food stalls.

Avenida Ashford
2 This major thoroughfare runs parallel to the shore and is San Juan's tourist strip. The road is lined with towering condominiums, hotels, restaurants, and upscale boutiques.

Watersports
3 The breezy beaches of Condado are ideal for watersports. Windsurfers *(left)* skim the waves here, kite-surfers perform aerial acrobatics, and parasailing *(see pp36–7)* is a fun way to get a bird's-eye view of the coast. Laguna del Condado is good for kayaking.

4 Laguna del Condado

Mangrove forests line the shores of this tidal saltwater lake inland of Condado. Each year, on June 23, the locals celebrate St. John, patron saint of the city, by plunging backward into the lake's waters 12 times for luck.

5 Juan Bobo Statue

This statue in Parque Antonia Quiñones portrays a legendary Puerto Rican *jíbaro* (farmer) trying to carry a basket of water *(left)*. The park – known to locals as *la placita de Condado* (Condado's plaza) – is a good place to get a taste of local life.

6 La Ventana al Mar

Lawns, contemporary sculptures, and a fountain make this waterfront plaza an attractive setting for the free folkloric performances held here.

7 Art Deco Architecture

Art Deco flourished in San Juan from 1930 to 1950, and Condado boasts many fine architectural examples *(above)*, especially along Avenidas Ashford and Magdalena.

Art Deco Heyday

Art Deco in Puerto Rico coincided with the great age of transport, and inspired local architects infused their buildings with slick, streamlined forms. Exteriors of most structures built between 1930 and 1950 feature distinctive Art Deco elements, such as rounded curves and horizontally banded parapets representing ships and trains moving through air.

8 Fine Restaurants

San Juan is lined with fine restaurants offering a variety of cuisines *(left)*. Many of the city's best restaurants are in Condado and Isla Verde, where upscale hotels lead the way *(see p65)*.

9 Ocean Park

Some of the area's best beaches are found in this classy residential neighborhood. Favored by beach-going youngsters, Ocean Park is also the setting for some of the trendiest hotels.

10 Casinos

Many deluxe hotels here have casinos, some of which are quite plush. Patrons, who must be at least 18 years old to enter, get dolled up in their *Miami Vice* best for a fun night out.

TOP 10 El Yunque

The 44-sq mile (114-sq km) El Yunque National Forest, formerly the Caribbean National Forest, is the only tropical rain forest within the US national park system. The rain-sodden wilderness rises to an elevation of 3,533 ft (1,075 m) at its highest point, Cerro El Toro, and features various ecosystems, including mountain cloudforest and dwarf forest on the highest slopes. The park has miles of hiking trails and spectacular waterfalls plunging down steep ravines. The region offers hikers some of the best bird-watching and wildlife-viewing on the island.

La Mina Trail signage

🕐 When picnicking, carry along your rain gear and use only designated sites. Avoid picnicking near forest streams due to the potential danger of flash floods.

🔵 The picnic sites have barbecue pits but you'll need to bring your own charcoal and meat to grill.

• Map M3
• El Yunque National Forest: 787 888 1880; open 7:30am–6pm; www.fs.fed.us/r8/el_yunque
• El Gran Portal Rain Forest Center: open 9am–4:30pm; adm $4; $2 for seniors; free for under-15s

Top 10 Features

1 El Gran Portal Rain Forest Center
2 Tropical Rain Forest
3 La Coca Waterfall
4 El Yunque Trail
5 Dwarf Forest
6 Sierra Palm Visitor Center
7 La Mina Trail
8 Birds
9 Picnics
10 Coquís

1 El Gran Portal Rain Forest Center

The main visitor center offers splendid interactive exhibits *(below)* on local geology, geography, and ecosystems. Pick up maps and literature on tropical forests here.

2 Tropical Rain Forest

Various types of subtropical rain forest *(main image)* carpet the lower- and mid-level slopes of El Yunque, with trees such as mahogany towering up to 164 ft (50 m). Their spreading crowns form a dense, broad canopy.

3 La Coca Waterfall

This is the first major attraction you come across in El Yunque. La Coca Waterfall *(right)* features a beautiful cascade tumbling 85 ft (26 m) onto boulder rocks. These can be slippery, so avoid the temptation to clamber.

4 El Yunque Trail

For the best views over the park (weather permitting), take this 2½-mile (4-km) trail *(left)* from the Palo Colorado Visitor Center. It climbs steeply through various ecosystems to El Yunque's summit, Cerro El Toro.

5 Dwarf Forest

Found at elevations above 3,280 ft (1,000 m), this elfin woodland is sodden by mists. The stunted trees rarely exceed 12 ft (3.5 m) in height.

6 Sierra Palm Visitor Center

This center displays a video introduction to the local ecosystems. Endemic Puerto Rican parrots are often seen outside the El Yunque Restaurant *(above)*.

8 Birds

A fabulous venue for bird-watchers *(see p36)*, El Yunque is home to many endemic bird species, including the endangered Puerto Rican parrot *(right)*, the Puerto Rican lizard cuckoo, and the elusive elfin wood warbler.

7 La Mina Trail

Follow the river along this downhill trail from the Palo Colorado Visitor Center to reach La Mina waterfall. It is one-way, but links with other trails.

What's in a Name?

The region was originally called *yuque*, after the Taíno god, Yuquiyu. Spanish conquistadores confused this with *yunque*, their word for anvil, and understandably so – the park's tallest peak, Cerro El Toro, is flat-topped and resembles an anvil when seen from a distance.

9 Picnics

Local families flock here on weekends and holidays to hike and picnic. Shaded benches, potable water, and rest rooms are located at the Palo Colorado and Sierra Palm Visitor Centers.

10 Coquís

These little frogs *(below)* are the national emblem and are named for their two-note chirp – "ko-KEE" – heard here at night. Puerto Rico has 16 species *(see p54)*.

TOP 10 Vieques

Vieques is the largest of the 24 isles and islets comprising the Spanish Virgin Islands, just off the east coast of Puerto Rico. Culturally and politically part of Puerto Rico, this tropical paradise moves to its own lackadaisical pace, drawing tourists seeking off-the-beaten-track charm. Hotels here are small-scale and trendy, and all-inclusive resorts are entirely absent. Vieques Wildlife Refuge offers nature-lovers plenty of thrills, not least as a nesting site for marine turtles. Much of the island is off-limits, following five decades in which it was a bombing range for the US Navy. However, its beaches are among the most gorgeous in Puerto Rico.

Laguna Kiani mangroves

🚲 A great way to explore the island is by bicycle. Rent a bike from Vieques Adventure Company *(see p105)*, or join a guided cycling tour.

🍴 While exploring Isabel Segunda, break for lunch at Bravo Beach Hotel (bbh) for the best of fine dining with a view *(see p99)*.

• Map N4–R4
• Vieques Art & History Museum: Calle Magnolia 471, Isabel Segunda: 787 741 1717; open 9:30am–5:30pm Wed–Sun
• Vieques Wildlife Refuge: 787 741 2138; open 6am–dark; www.fws.gov/caribbean/refuges/vieques
• Siddhia Hutchinson Art Gallery: Calle 3, Isabel Segunda: 787 741 1343; open 10am–4pm Mon–Sat, noon–3pm Sun

Top 10 Features

1. Esperanza
2. Isabel Segunda
3. Fort Conde Mirasol and Vieques Art & History Museum
4. Bahía Bioluminiscente
5. Vieques Wildlife Refuge
6. Green Beach
7. Blue Beach
8. Siddhia Hutchinson Art Gallery
9. Scuba Diving
10. Laguna Kiani

Esperanza
This former sugar port, now a sleepy hamlet, overlooks a scenic bay that is popular with yachters *(main image)*. Its scrub-covered, shorefront hills are home to several boutique hotels.

Isabel Segunda
Most of the isle's 9,000 or so people live in this small town, which remains charmingly old world and has little traffic. The town's lighthouse *(left)*, built in 1896, adds to its charm.

Fort Conde Mirasol and Vieques Art & History Museum
This hilltop fort, built in the 1840s, was the last Spanish fort constructed in the Americas. It now houses the Vieques Art & History Museum, which has displays from pre-Columbian times through the island's colonial years *(right)*.

Bahía Bioluminiscente
This bay *(above)* seems to come alive at night – bioluminescent micro-organisms glow when the water is disturbed. Go on a kayak trip to see for yourself *(see p110)*.

Vieques Wildlife Refuge
Covering 28 sq miles (72 sq km), this preserve protects beaches, coastal lagoons, mangrove wetlands, and upland semi-deciduous forests.

Green Beach
This strip of white sand fringes turquoise, coral-filled waters that are great for snorkeling and kayaking *(below)*. Beware currents that can pull swimmers into the Pasaje de Vieques channel.

Blue Beach
Once a setting for the US Navy's amphibious assault manoeuvers, this stunning beach *(below)* is now entirely peaceful. Rent a kayak and row out to a serene cay.

Siddhia Hutchinson Art Gallery
The studio-gallery *(left)* of local artist Siddhia Hutchinson is a good place to purchase prints, textiles, and ceramics inspired by the natural world of Puerto Rico.

Red Flag Day
Vieques was used for decades by the US Navy for gunnery practice. On days when shooting was in progress, red flags were hoisted to warn locals that the beaches were off limits. The residents protested for years, and the disagreement came to a head in 1999 after a local guard was killed by an errant bomb. The bombardment ceased in 2003 when the navy pulled out of Vieques.

Scuba Diving
Dive sites off the south shore include Blue Tank Reef, a 2-mile (3-km) coral reef in clear waters, and Las Tres Rocas, where the reef is packed with corals and sponges and inhabited by moray eels.

Laguna Kiani
This wetland ecosystem comprises a large mangrove forest. Manatees *(see p54)* can sometimes be seen in the water here, and bulldog bats skim the surface for fish at night.

For information on excursions to Vieques See p110.

TOP10 Culebra

The second largest of the Spanish Virgin Islands, this somnolent crab-claw-shaped island is renowned for its scintillating beaches, including indisputably Puerto Rico's finest: Playa Flamenco, a popular weekend getaway for locals from the main island, who arrive by ferry from Fajardo. The island is indented with pristine, sandy coves where marine turtles come ashore to lay eggs – an annual ritual that also occurs on the unpopulated outlying isles that make up much of Culebra National Wildlife Refuge. Culebra's many offshore coral reefs are a delight for snorkelers and divers to explore.

A souvenir kiosk at Dewey

🍺 **The Dinghy Dock (787 742 0233) is a good place to mingle with locals and boaters over a cool beer and fresh, delicious seafood.**

• Map Q3–R3
• Culebra National Wildlife Refuge: 787 742 0115; open 7am–4:30pm; www.fws.gov/caribbean/refuges/culebra

Top 10 Features

1. Dewey
2. Playa Flamenco
3. Marine Turtles
4. Playa Soldado
5. Playa Carlos Rosario
6. Playa Brava
7. Culebra National Wildlife Refuge
8. Cayo Luis Peña
9. Culebrita
10. Bonefishing

Dewey

The island's only town is named for the US admiral who seized Culebra in 1898. Visitors – both male and female – are expected to wear a shirt while exploring the town, on pain of a fine.

Playa Flamenco

This broad sweep of pure-white sand draws day-trippers from the main island on weekends. The sensational beach is washed by powerful ocean waters good for surfing. World War II Sherman tanks *(below)* add interest.

Marine Turtles

Four species of marine turtles – green, hawksbill, leatherback, and loggerhead – crawl ashore to nest from April through August on the beaches, notably along the north shore and on Culebrita.

Playa Soldado
The coral reef at this rocky beach, a snorkeler's delight, is only 66 ft (20 m) from shore and 10 ft (3 m) beneath the calm surface *(above)*.

Playa Carlos Rosario
This beach, connected to Playa Flamenco by a hiking trail, has a coral reef within a few feet of shore and is popular with yachters. Water-taxis run here from Dewey.

Playa Brava
A remote beach accessible by dirt road from the southeast side of the island's airport, Angry Beach is named for the rough waves that pound ashore. The sands are protected as a marine turtle nesting site.

Culebra National Wildlife Refuge
Covering a quarter of the island, this 245-sq mile (627-sq km) wildlife refuge protects breeding habitats of marine turtles, manatees *(above)*, and avian species, such as red-billed tropic birds.

Cayo Luis Peña
A craggy coral cay, Cayo Luis Peña is an important habitat for seabirds, including red-billed tropic birds. It is enclosed by a fringing reef, with sheltered waters that are excellent for snorkeling.

Culebrita
This tiny uninhabited isle, half-a-mile (1 km) east of Culebra, has beautiful beaches shelving into electric-blue waters. It is perfect for picnicking and snorkeling. Water-taxis *(below)* will ferry you from Dewey.

Bonefishing
The reef-protected, crystal-clear, sand-bottomed shallows of Culebra are an angler's delight. Silvery, well-camouflaged bonefish look easily, but once caught on the line, put up a fight to remember.

Leatherback Turtles

The critically endangered leatherback turtle is found in all the world's oceans, and travels great distances using its thick layer of fat for insulation in cold waters. Unlike other turtle species, it has no external skeleton or shell. Its streamlined body is covered by a leathery skin, hence the name. Females lay their eggs on tropical beaches, like those of Puerto Rico.

For information on excursions to Culebra See p110.

Parque de las Cavernas del Río Camuy

This park comprises part of the world's third-largest cave system, Cavernas del Río Camuy, which has more than 220 underground caverns. One of the chambers is so large, it could swallow a 30-story building. Spotlights illuminate fantastic stalactites, stalagmites, and other dripstone formations, some of which are etched with pre-Columbian Taíno motifs. Bats flit about overhead, tarantulas crawl underfoot, and a blind endemic fish species swims in the underground river, Río Camuy. These caves were only discovered in the 1950s and are today under the care of Puerto Rico's Compañia de Parques Nacionales.

A walkway to the caves

🐾 The walkways can get slippery, so wear comfortable shoes with good grip. A sweater or light jacket can come in handy against the chill of the caverns.

🍴 The visitor center has a snack bar and the gift shop sells snacks. A campsite in the park has toilets and showers.

• Map D3
• Carretera 129 Km 20, Camuy
• 787 898 3100
• Open 8:30am–5pm Wed–Sun and holidays
• Adm $15 for adults; $10 for children (4–12 years)

Top 10 Features

1 Cueva Clara de Enpalma
2 Taíno Pictographs
3 Dripstone Formations
4 Trolley Ride
5 Tres Pueblo Sinkhole
6 Bats
7 Río Camuy
8 Tarantulas
9 Cueva Catedral
10 Visitor Center

1 Cueva Clara de Enpalma

This massive cavern soars 170 ft (52 m) high and extends lengthways for more than 1,970 ft (600 m) to a vast sinkhole – the Sumidero Enpalma *(below)*. Concrete paths snake along the cavern's floor, providing a fascinating loop trail.

2 Taíno Pictographs

Ancient indigenous people daubed symbolic spiritual figures onto the cave walls using mixtures of charcoal, bat droppings, and animal fat. These have survived millennia thanks to the natural humidity and coolness of the caverns.

3 Dripstone Formations

Many of the stalactites *(right)*, stalagmites, and other calcite formations in the caves resemble familiar shapes, such as animals and church organs. Visitors will have fun identifying the forms, some of which are floodlit.

An hour-long guided tour takes visitors to 16 of the caves.

4 Trolley Ride
Your visit begins with a ride in a trolley *(above)* that snakes downhill past bamboo and banana trees to the cave entrance. The return journey passes by the Tres Pueblo Sinkhole.

5 Tres Pueblo Sinkhole
This massive depression *(main image)* plunges 400 ft (120 m) and was formed when the ceiling of an underground cavern collapsed. The Río Camuy at its base can be seen emerging from one cavern and entering another.

6 Bats
More than 100,000 bats roost in the caves, where they cling to rooftop crevices by day, before swarming out in hordes at dusk to forage for insects.

7 Río Camuy
This river weaves its way through the cave system. It has been carving out the subterranean landscape for millions of years, assisted by rainwater that seeps into the limestone, weakening the structural joints *(below)*.

8 Tarantulas
These huge, hairy, long-legged spiders are numerous in the cool, damp interior of the caves. They play an important part in the local ecology and are harmless unless provoked.

9 Cueva Catedral
This cavern *(below)* contains more than 40 pre-Columbian pictographs. Reaching the entrance requires a rappel down a rock wall and should be arranged with local tour operators.

10 Visitor Center
Information panels are on display in the timber-and-fieldstone visitor center. A short film on the cavern system and its formation is shown prior to the guided tour.

Sacred Caverns
The Taíno never lived in caves, which they considered sacred portals to the spirit world. They drew pictures of fearsome gods to guard the entrances, and only high-ranking community figures, like shamans, were allowed to enter. These people believed that their ancestral spirits lived in caves and only emerged at night to eat fruits. Legend has it that the spirits were so occupied in gorging themselves that they were still outside the caves when the sun came up, turning them into human beings.

TOP 10 Centro Ceremonial Indígena de Tibes

This archaeological site in the hills on the northern outskirts of Ponce is the most important pre-Columbian site in Puerto Rico. Remarkably, it was only unearthed in 1975, when devastating floods exposed extensive Taíno ruins that notably include bateyes (ball courts), burial grounds, and granite boulders etched with petroglyphs. The ruins date back about 2,000 years and form the only known site also occupied by the Igneris – a pre-Taíno tribe about which little is known, except that they were overrun by the Taíno (see p30) in around AD 1000. The site is still being excavated.

Main entrance of the park

🕐 Be sure to make a reservation before you visit the park, as tours often sell out and you cannot explore the site unaccompanied.

🍴 A small café here serves snacks. There are also picnic benches by the river, so consider bringing your own lunch to enjoy under the shade trees.

- Map F5
- Carretera 503 Km 2.8
- 787 840 2255
- Open 8am–3:30pm Tue–Sun
- Adm $3 for adults; $2 for children (5–12 years); $1.50 for seniors
- Visits are by guided tour only; reservations are recommended.

Top 10 Features

1. Cemí
2. Petroglyphs
3. Bateyes
4. Museum
5. Guided Tour
6. Ceramics
7. Replica Village
8. Botanical Garden
9. Star-Shaped Plaza
10. Cemetery

1 Cemí
These sacred effigies of Taíno gods *(below)*, in the form of wooden and stone statuettes, were believed to be empowered. *Cemí* were created and worshipped by the Taíno to bless the land with good harvests, and its people with fertility and health.

2 Petroglyphs
The Taíno etched large rocks here with depictions of spiritual figures, including one of a bat – the Taíno messenger of death. Many of the rock are believed to have been transported from far away.

3 Bateyes
These plazas of paved stone *(right)* were used for ball games and ceremonial dances. Tibes has 12 *bateyes* – each is about the size of a basketball court and is ringed by large boulders.

4 Museum

The small on-site museum's exhibits *(right)* include axe-heads, pottery, *cemí*, and even a skeleton, all of which were excavated here. A 30-minute video helps put the displays in perspective.

5 Guided Tour

A 90-minute guided tour takes you through sub-tropical forest, a replica village, and the *bateyes*, as the guide explains aspects of indigenous life. Re-enactments in costumes *(right)* are also occasionally staged.

6 Ceramics

Hundreds of interesting Igneri and Taíno ceramics have been unearthed here, including pots *(below)*, *cemí*, and headless figures with their hands tied behind their backs, suggesting execution.

7 Replica Village

A reconstruction of a *yucayeque* (Taíno village) *(main image)* features a rectangular *caney* (the village chief's house) and circular, thatched *bohíos* (huts that were used by the villagers). These help visitors understand the Taíno way of life.

8 Botanical Garden

Tibes features a garden of plants and trees that were used by the Taíno. These include yucca, tobacco, and corn, as well as the local *guanábana*, *higüero*, and calabash, a large gourd *(left)*.

9 Star-Shaped Plaza

One of the *bateyes* is, as its name implies, shaped like a star. It is thought to have been used as an astronomical compass, with stones laid in the form of triangles corresponding to cardinal points in the universe.

10 Cemetery

The main *batey* was built atop a cemetery, where 186 skeletons from both the Igneri and Taíno cultures were found. Most were curled into a fetal position, in the belief that they would be reborn.

Ball Games

The Taíno played violent ritual ball games in which competing teams could use any part of their body, except their hands. The balls were solid and players wore protective pads. The games were played for sport as well as for diversion, religious purposes, and even to make judicial decisions, including whether prisoners of war should be freed or killed.

For more on Puerto Rico's history **See pp30–31.**

TOP 10 San Germán

This quaint hillside town, known locally as "Ciudad de las Lomas" (City of the Hills), was founded in 1573 and boasts the island's most intact colonial core outside Old San Juan. Its leafy plazas are surrounded by exquisite colonial buildings in eclectic architectural styles – reminders of the wealth generated by the 19th-century coffee boom. In all, the 36-acre (15-ha) historic core has 249 buildings listed on the National Register of Historic Places, including a 400-year-old church, Iglesia Porta Coeli, containing the nation's most important religious art museum. The town is named after Germaine de Foix, the second wife of King Ferdinand of Spain.

Casa Acosta y Forés

🐾 Wear good walking shoes and carry water – the town is hilly and exploring the streets can be very hard work.

🍴 The town's Mike's Steak House *(see p79)* is a good place to dine on some excellent chargrilled steak and seafood.

• Map C5
• San Germán Tourism and Culture Office: Interamerican University Avenue; 787 892 3790; open 8am–4pm Mon–Fri
• Casa Morales: Calle Ramos 38
• Casa Lola Rodríguez de Tió: Calle Dr Santiago Veve 13
• Iglesia de San Germán de Auxerre: Plaza Francisco Mariano Quiñones; 787 892 1027
• Casa Acosta y Forés: Calle Dr Santiago Veve 70
• Casa Juan Ortíz Perichi: Calle Luna 94

Top 10 Features

1. Plaza Santo Domingo
2. Iglesia Porta Coeli
3. Porta Coeli Religious Art Museum
4. Casa Morales
5. Plaza Francisco Mariano Quiñones
6. Casa Lola Rodríguez de Tió
7. Iglesia de San Germán de Auxerre
8. Evening Paseo
9. Casa Acosta y Forés
10. Casa Juan Ortíz Perichi

2 Iglesia Porta Coeli
The simple Spanish-mission style "Heaven's Gate" church *(above)* dates from 1606 and stands atop a stepped, red-bricked pedestal. Originally a monastery, it was fortified to guard against pirates.

Porta Coeli Religious Art Museum 3
The Museo de Arte Religioso, within the Iglesia Porta Coeli, exhibits religious statuary, precious paintings *(right)*, and the nation's largest collection of *santos* (statues of saints) *(see p33).*

1 Plaza Santo Domingo
The elongated Plaza Santo Domingo, once a market-place, is paved with red brick and lined with historic buildings and attractively restored, Victorian-inspired, 19th-century mansions.

4 Casa Morales
The Victorian-inspired photogenic Casa Morales *(main image)*, a private residence built in 1898, stands on a corner of Plaza Santo Domingo. Its design reflects the US influence on the island.

5 Plaza Francisco Mariano Quiñones
This oblong square, a popular spot for locals to gather and gossip, features topiary and is graced by wrought-iron benches and an 18th-century church.

6 Casa Lola Rodríguez de Tió
Built in the 17th century, this mansion was occupied by family members of explorer Ponce de León *(see p30)*, and by patriot-poet Lola Rodríguez de Tió (1843–1924), who designed the Puerto Rican flag.

7 Iglesia de San Germán de Auxerre
This Neo Classical church, which rises over Plaza Francisco Mariano Quiñones, was completed in 1848. It boasts an impressive crystal chandelier *(below)* and trompe l'oeil.

8 Evening Paseo
Locals gather at dusk to promenade along the town's twin plazas, both of which have cobblestone streets and shady trees that lend San Germán a romantic yesteryear air.

9 Casa Acosta y Forés
Considered one of the most beautiful homes in Puerto Rico, this mansion exemplifies the island's Art Nouveau architecture era with its Victorian-inspired elements.

Pirate Past
Supposedly, many of San Germán's wealthy inhabitants derived their income as pirates, or as wreckers who lured ships onto the rocks, although this is more apocryphal than fact. The township was founded in 1511 at the mouth of the Río Guaorabo, but attacks by French corsairs in 1528, 1538, and 1554 forced the residents to re-establish their town at the present site.

10 Casa Juan Ortíz Perichi
Built in 1920, this home, which is one block south of Plaza Santo Domingo, is a classic example of ornamental architecture and features elegantly curved balconies and a pitched roof *(above)*.

TOP 10 Museo de Arte de Ponce

The superb exhibits at this world-class museum range from works by Goya, Rubens, Van Dyck, and Rodin to avant-garde Puerto Rican artists and span Western art from the Middle Ages to the 19th century. The permanent collection comprises more than 4,000 paintings, sculptures, and works on paper. Much of it was amassed over four decades, beginning in 1957, by Don Luis A. Ferré, former governor and patron of the arts. The museum, which boasts 30 galleries, also features temporary exhibitions and works on loan. A two-year, multi-million-dollar renovation was completed in 2010, which doubled the capacity of the building.

Charles Frederick Ulrich's The Glass Blowers

🎨 **Kids in tow?** Special family tours and workshops are held most Saturdays – these are a great way to foster art appreciation in children.

🚫 No food or drink is allowed on the premises, but there is a restaurant and cyber café (see website for details).

• Map F5
• Av Las Américas 2325
• 787 848 0505
• Open 10am–6pm Wed–Mon
• Adm $6 for adults; $3 for children (under 12 years), seniors and students
• www.museoarte ponce.org
• Guided tours 11am–2pm daily or by appointment; audio guides are available for $2.

Top 10 Features

1. The Building
2. Vestibule
3. Temporary Exhibits
4. The Pre-Raphaelites
5. Flaming June
6. Puerto Rican Art
7. Italian Art
8. North American Art
9. Sculptures
10. Permanent Collection Storage Space

1 The Building
Completed in 1965, the Museo de Arte de Ponce is housed in a two-story modernist structure designed by Edward Durell Stone. It has hexagonal galleries with ceilings of hexagonal skylights.

2 Vestibule
The museum's lobby features a glass entrance and a light-filled circular atrium. The upper level is accessed by two sweeping staircases *(below)*. The centerpiece is an eye-catching sculpture by Rodin.

3 Temporary Exhibits
The museum shows an active calendar of exhibitions featuring European Old Masters and international contemporary art. These have included an exhibition on muralist Diego Rivera (1886–1957), as well as *The Age of Rodin* and *The Santos Tradition in Puerto Rican*, which displayed wooden saints *(see p47)* – the hallmark of Puerto Rican popular art.

4 The Pre-Raphaelites

The paintings in the Pre-Raphaelite gallery are superb examples of this British school. Among them are Edward Burne-Jones's masterpiece, *The Last Sleep of Arthur in Avalon*, and works by Dante Gabriel Rossetti and John Everett Millais.

6 Puerto Rican Art

Puerto Rico's finest artists, such as José Campeche and Francisco Oller, are well represented in works spanning the 18th century to the present day.

5 Flaming June

The museum's sensual showpiece *(above)*, *Flaming June* is Lord Frederic Leighton's Classicist-inspired, Victorian-era masterpiece of a damsel in a flaming orange robe languorously basking in the Mediterranean sun.

MUSEO DE ARTE

7 Italian Art

The Italian masters are found on the first and second floors of the main building. They focus on the Baroque period, with a fine collection of Florentine School pieces by Bernardo Strozzi *(above)*, Francesco Furini, and Luca Giordano.

Edward Durell Stone

A renowned American architect, Stone (1902–78) was an early exponent of modernism and later of the post-modernist style. His first major commission was the lobby and grand ballroom of the Waldorf-Astoria hotel in New York City, where he also designed Radio City Music Hall and the Museum of Modern Art. Stone is also acclaimed for Washington, D.C.'s Kennedy Center for the Performing Arts.

8 North American Art

Frederic Edwin Church's *Morning in the Tropics* (1872) and *The Glass Blowers* (1883) by Charles Frederick Ulrich are highlights of this collection, which also includes pieces by George Inness.

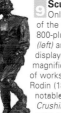

9 Sculptures

Only a fraction of the museum's 800-plus sculptures *(left)* are currently displayed, including a magnificent collection of works by Auguste Rodin (1840–1917). His notable piece, *Apollo Crushing the Serpent*, was acquired by the museum in 1962.

10 Permanent Collection Storage Space

Situated in the annex, this storage space is open to the public. It offers visitors the opportunity to view artworks from the permanent collection that are not officially on display.

A depiction of the Haitian rebellion

Top 10 Moments in History

1 First Settlers
It is thought that Puerto Rico's earliest settlers may have arrived from Florida about 5,000 years ago. These hunter-gatherers were later displaced by the Igneris, an Arawak tribe from the Orinoco basin of South America.

2 Taíno Arrival
After a long migration up the Caribbean chain, the Taíno people arrived on the island, which they called Borinquen, in around 500 BC. This peaceful society lived on fishing and farming, worshipped gods of nature, and lived in villages led by chieftains.

3 Columbus' Arrival
The Genovese explorer first set foot on the island during his second voyage in 1493, and christened it San Juan Bautista. His discovery led to Spanish rule of the island and the rapid enslavement of the Taíno. By 1521, the island had been renamed Puerto Rico – Rich Port – by conquistador Ponce de León.

4 San Juan Founded
In 1521 the first Spanish settlement, Caparra, was abandoned and Ponce de León established a new town on a peninsula that protected a huge bay. San Juan was constantly under pirate raids and was briefly occupied by English forces in 1598. Fortifications were added to safeguard the port.

5 Haitian Rebellion
A slave rebellion in Haiti in 1791 led to the demise of the island's French sugar trade. Fears of a similar uprising in Puerto Rico prompted Spain to loosen the island's restrictive trade laws, resulting in an economic boom as US investors poured money into the sugar industry.

6 El Grito de Lares
The *criollo* (island born) craved independence from Spain, but nationalist aspirations were brutally suppressed. *Independentistas* launched "The Cry of Lares" *(see p68)* in September 1869, which resulted in liberal reforms.

7 The Fight for Autonomy
In 1895 Puerto Rican exiles allied with Cuban nationalists during Cuba's second war of independence from Spain. A liberal government took over in Spain and

A mural depicting Columbus' arrival in Puerto Rico

Preceding pages **El Yunque rain forest, Puerto Rico**

Fiftieth anniversary as a US Commonwealth

Luis Muñoz Rivera petitioned for Puerto Rican autonomy. On July 17, 1898 an independent legislature convened.

8 US Take-Over
Covetous of Spain's colonies, the US found a pretext to declare war on the country on April 25, 1898. San Juan was bombarded by US warships and marines landed at Guánica. Spain sued for peace and the US took control of Puerto Rico.

9 Citizenship Granted
US investors poured money into Puerto Rico, which was ruled by governors imposed by Washington. Although Puerto Ricans were granted US citizenship in 1917, self-government was denied, spawning a nationalist movement that culminated in an assassination attempt in 1950 against President Truman.

10 Commonwealth Status
On July 25, 1952, the island became the Commonwealth of Puerto Rico, with its own anthem, flag, and judiciary. Islanders, however, could still not vote for the US president. The economy subsequently witnessed a boom-and-bust cycle and the island became dependent on federal subsidies and US investments.

Top 10 Famous Puerto Ricans

1 Luis Muñoz Rivera (1859–1916)
Poet and political activist who was instrumental in gaining autonomy for Puerto Rico.

2 Luis Muñoz Marín (1898–1980)
The first democratically elected governor of Puerto Rico and considered the "Father of Modern Puerto Rico."

3 Raúl Juliá (1940–94)
Award-winning actor best-known for his roles in the hits *Addams Family* and *Kiss of the Spider Woman*.

4 Eugenio María de Hostos (1839–1903)
Liberal lawyer and independence activist who helped establish Puerto Rico's education system.

5 Jimmy Smits (b. 1955)
New York-born actor who starred in *Star Wars*, *Miami Vice*, and *L.A. Law*.

6 Ramón Power y Giralt (1775–1813)
An admiral in the Spanish navy who represented Puerto Rico in the Spanish Cortes.

7 Geraldo Rivera (b. 1943)
Attorney, television reporter, and host of *The Geraldo Rivera Show*.

8 Wilfred Benítez (b. 1958)
Boxer who won world championships in three separate weight divisions.

9 Jennifer López (b. 1969)
Singer and actress born in New York *(see p34)*.

10 Juan 'Chi Chi' Rodríguez (b. 1935)
Professional golfer who was inducted into the World Golf Hall of Fame.

Left **Interior of the Porta Coeli Religious Art Museum** Right **Museo de las Américas' facade**

🔟 Museums

1 Instituto de Cultura Puertorriqueña

The headquarters of the nation's main cultural organization is in an imposing 19th-century Neo-Classical building. Its galleries display exhibits on geology, pre-Columbian relics and religious icons, colonial miscellany, and contemporary art *(see p9)*.

2 Museo Pablo Casals

Casals *(see p34)*, the Spanish cellist who lived his last 15 years in San Juan, is honored in this 18th-century town house on Plaza San José. Exhibits include his cello and original manuscripts *(see p62)*.

Casals' cello at Museo Pablo Casals

3 Museo de Arte de Puerto Rico

Housed in a former Neo-Classical hospital and adjoining modernist structure, this museum showcases works by Puerto Rico's foremost artists from the 16th century onward. A sculpture garden features avant-garde works *(see pp60–61)*.

4 Museo de San Juan

Art and artifacts tracing the city's history are displayed in this former colonial-era marketplace. Audio-visual exhibits provide a lively overview of the past. ⬡ *Map U5 • Calle Norzagaray 150, San Juan • 787 724 1875 • Open 9am–4pm Tue–Fri, 10am–4pm Sat–Sun*

5 Museo de las Américas

This museum, in the former Spanish military headquarters, celebrates the many cultures of the Americas. Its display of Latin American folk art and religious icons includes a collection of *santos (see p47)*. ⬡ *Map T5 • Cuartel de Ballajá, Calle Norzagaray, San Juan • 787 724 5052 • Open 9am–noon & 1–4pm Tue–Sat, noon–5pm Sun • Adm*

6 Museo de Arte de Ponce

Works by Dutch, English, French, and Italian masters, North American artists, and Puerto Rico's foremost painters are housed in this art museum, itself an architectural masterpiece, designed by modernist Edward Durell Stone *(see pp26–7)*.

Elegant staircases in the Museo de Arte de Puerto Rico

7 Vieques Art & History Museum

This thoughtfully put-together museum traces Vieques' past and has fine exhibits on the clash of the Spanish and Taíno cultures, as well as antique weaponry. It also offers profiles of local flora and fauna *(see p16)*.

8 Angel Ramos Foundation Visitor Center

Making sense of the Arecibo observatory is made easy at this superb facility, which has educational panels, audio-visual displays, and interactive exhibits on atmospheric science, astronomy, and the operation of the radio telescope *(see p67)*.

Museo de la História de Ponce

9 Museo de la História de Ponce

The ten galleries in this Moorish-inspired mansion with a modern annex explore the city's past and current daily life. Oddities include a marble bathtub once owned by Samuel Morse, inventor of the Morse code *(see p86)*.

10 Porta Coeli Religious Art Museum

A wealth of religious icons, from precious 18th- and 19th-century paintings and sculptures to the island's foremost collection of *santos (see p47)*, are displayed in Puerto Rico's oldest chapel.
🕲 *Map C5 • Plaza Santo Domingo, San Germán • 787 892 5845 • Open 9am–noon & 1–4pm Thu–Sun*

Top 10 Taíno Cultural Sights

1 Parque Ceremonial Indígena Caguana
A ceremonial site with ten *bateyes* and impressive petroglyphs *(see p68)*.

2 Centro Ceremonial Indígena de Tibes
The most extensive site in Puerto Rico, with a recreated Taíno village *(see pp22–3)*.

3 Vieques Art & History Museum
Displays pre-Columbian artifacts and explores the Spanish decimation of local culture *(see p16)*.

4 La Cueva del Indio
This group of rocks forming grottoes features more than 200 petroglyphs.
🕲 *Map M4 • Las Piedras • 787 733 2160 ext. 2474 • Guided tours: 8am–4pm Mon–Fri*

5 Instituto de Cultura Puertorriqueña
A gallery here displays Taíno relics excavated from sites around the island *(see p9)*.

6 Museo de las Américas
Exhibits of pre-Columbian culture from throughout the Americas, including dug-out canoes *(see opposite)*.

7 Petroglyphs
Symbols of *cemí* and other spiritual figures carved into rocks all over Puerto Rico.

8 Re-Enactments
Indigenous life is re-enacted at a replica village at Tibes *(see p23)*.

9 Jácana
This site near Ponce has many *bateyes* that await excavation. 🕲 *Map F5*

10 Museo Indígena Cemí
A collection of *cemí* and petroglyphs, which can also be seen in situ nearby *(see p92)*.

➡ *For more on Puerto Rico's history See pp30–31.*

Left **José Feliciano performing** Right **Pablo Casals**

Musicians

Pablo Casals (1876–1973)

Spanish-born Casals began playing musical instruments at the age of four. He made his debut at Carnegie Hall in 1904 and thereafter built a reputation as the world's premier cellist. He settled in Puerto Rico in 1956, where he later established the annual Casals Festival (see p42).

Santos Colón (1922–98)

This salsa singer, also known as "Santito," produced many popular albums. He also performed with Tito Puente's orchestra, with whom he contributed the easily recognizable "Aha! Aha!" in the original version of the song *Oye Como Va*. Colón is best known for his haunting bolero songs and Spanish interpretations of English-language classics.

Tito Puente (1923–2000)

Born in New York to Puerto Rican parents, Ernesto Antonio Puente studied at the Julliard School of Music after serving in the US Navy during World War II. He helped popularize mambo, and later, salsa, and earned the nickname "King of Latin Music" for his sensuous, fast-paced mambo and Latin-jazz compositions. He won five Grammy Awards.

José Feliciano (b. 1945)

Feliciano, a blind guitarist from Lares, began performing professionally at 17. He had huge hits with bolero and folk-pop-soul albums, and in 1969 won Grammy Awards for Best New Artist of the Year and for Best Pop Song of the Year. His most famous album is *Felíz Navidad*.

Jennifer Lopez (b. 1969)

This multi-talented entertainer, nicknamed J.Lo, enjoys great success as a singer, song-writer, and actress. She has sold more than 50 million albums worldwide and has her own perfume brand and fashion line. She married Marc Anthony in 2004, but the couple divorced in 2011.

Marc Anthony (b. 1968)

A singer-songwriter and actor, Marc Anthony has crossover success in both English and Spanish markets for his salsa and Latin-pop renditions. He started as a back-up singer and released his first album in 1993.

Jennifer Lopez and Marc Anthony

*Sign up for DK's email newsletter on **traveldk.com***

Ricky Martin

7 Ricky Martin (b. 1971)
Born Enrique Martín Morales, this Latin pop singer rose to fame as a member of the boy band Menudo. Since going solo in 1991, he has had more than 20 top-ten singles.

8 Tito Rodríguez (1923–73)
Rodríguez, a singer-songwriter born in Santurce, formed his own band in the 1940s, studied at the Julliard School in New York, and later earned the nickname "El Inolvidable" (The Unforgettable) for his version of a Cuban song with that name. His mambo renditions were huge successes in the 1950s.

9 Maxwell (b. 1973)
This R & B artist, christened Gerard Maxwell Menard, rose to fame playing the New York club scene. His single, *Fortunate*, was the top-selling US R & B song of 1999. He has been nominated for five Grammy Awards.

10 Tony Orlando (b. 1944)
Raised in New York by a Puerto Rican mother and Greek father, Orlando formed the band Dawn, known for such 1970s hits as *Knock Three Times*. He later hosted television's first multi-ethnic variety show.

Top 10 Beauty Queens

1 Marisol Malaret (b. 1949)
After winning the Miss Puerto Rico and Miss Universe 1970 titles, Malaret became a TV host.

2 Wilnelia Merced (b. 1959)
Winner of the Miss World 1975 title, Merced married TV entertainer Bruce Forsyth.

3 Deborah Carthy-Deu (b. 1966)
This ballerina became Miss Puerto Rico 1985 and was then crowned Miss Universe.

4 Laurie Tamara Simpson (b. 1967)
This blonde Miss Puerto Rico 1987 later won the Miss International title.

5 Dayanara Torres (b. 1974)
Torres won the Miss Universe title in 1993 and later married Marc Anthony.

6 Denise Quiñones (b. 1980)
In 2001, Quiñones became the fourth Puerto Rican winner of the Miss Universe title.

7 Susie Castillo (b. 1980)
A teen model, Castillo held the Miss USA 2003 title and has been an MTV host.

8 Cynthia Olavarria (b. 1982)
Olavarria won her first beauty title at 11 and was crowned Miss Puerto Rico in 2004.

9 Ingrid Marie Rivera (b. 1983)
Placed third in the 2005 Miss World contest, Rivera was Miss Puerto Rico in 2008.

10 Zuleyka Rivera (b. 1987)
This actress won the Miss Puerto Rico and Miss Universe titles in 2006.

Left **Swimming at Playa Flamenco** Center **Bird-watching** Right **A golf course on the west coast**

🔟 Outdoor Activities

Cycling
Although heavy traffic makes cycling unsafe in most urban areas on the island, the countryside is less intimidating and offers the reward of spectacular scenery. Bikes can be hired from specialist tour operators, who also help plan exciting excursions.
🚲 *Hot Dog Cycling, San Juan: 787 791 0776; www.hotdog cycling.com • Rent the Bicycle, Old San Juan: 787 602 9696*

Sport Fishing
Anglers rave about the quality of deep-sea fishing off Puerto Rico, where tuna, wahoo, and white and blue marlin are among the prize catches. Fishing charters are offered from most seafront towns. Fly-fishing for bass, bonefish, and tarpon is also popular – a license is required *(see p110)*.

Exploring on a bike

Scuba Diving
Healthy coral reefs ring the island and the Puerto Rico Trench off the south coast offers fantastic wall dives. Vieques and Culebra are also popular and have plane- and shipwrecks for divers to explore. Diving is possible year-round – many resorts and dive operators offer training courses *(see p110)*.

Golfing
Puerto Rico is a world-class golf destination with more than 23 courses designed by celebrity golfers. Most are ocean-front courses associated with large resort hotels, although all are also open for public play.

Surfing
Surf aficionados proclaim Rincón to be one of the world's finest surf spots, with waves topping 33 ft (10 m) in winter *(see p110)*. Aguadilla *(see p78)* and Playa de Jobos *(see p68)* also offer superb surfing, while the beaches of Dorado *(see p67)* and Luquillo *(see p96)* are good for beginners.

Swimming
Many of Puerto Rico's beautiful beaches *(see pp38–9)* are protected from rough waves by coral reefs, but strong under-tows are potential dangers. It is wise to check the swimming conditions with the locals before you step into the waters.

Windsurfing and parasailing

Hiking through Bosque Estatal de Guánica

Hiking
Puerto Rico's mountainous interior is ideal hiking terrain, with El Yunque (see pp14–15), which boasts a variety of trails, being the most popular place. Bosque Estatal de Guánica (see p83) offers relatively flat trails that are good for beginners.

Parasailing
Popular at the north-coast resorts, parasailing involves attaching yourself to a harness and giant kite. You are then towed by a speedboat and rise upward, gaining an exhilarating bird's-eye view of the coastline.

Bird-Watching
With 350 bird species, the island brings bird-watchers flocking. Spotting birds in the island's national parks and preserves is easy, especially with an experienced guide close at hand (see p110).

Spelunking
The island is riddled with caverns, and spelunking (caving) is a popular activity. Some caves require rappel access and many are prone to flash flooding, so explore with a reputed adventure company. Aventuras Tierra Adentro: 787 766 0470; www.aventuraspr.com
• Rocaliza Adventure Tour Company: 787 268 0101; www.rocaliza.com

Top 10 Nature Trails

1 Bosque Estatal Cambalache
A hiker's delight with eight trails, a bike trail, and camping facilities (see p69).

2 Bosque Estatal de Guajataca
Twenty-five miles (40 km) of trails through dramatic karst landscapes (see pp68–9).

3 Kayak Trail
A kayak trail that penetrates the mangrove-lined estuaries of Bahía de Jobos preserve.

4 Bosque Estatal de Guánica
A dry forest with 36 miles (58 km) of trails through four ecosystems (see p83).

5 El Yunque Trail
A climb from Palo Colorado Visitor Center to El Yunque's summit (see p15).

6 Paseo Piñones Recreational Trail
A paved coastal trail for walkers, bicyclists, and roller-skaters. Map L2

7 Playa Carlos Rosario Trail
A short trail leading over an isthmus separating Playa Flamenco and Playa Carlos Rosario. Map Q3

8 Culebra National Wildlife Refuge
A trail with boulders studding dry forest and leading to Playa Resaca (see p19).

9 Bosque Estatal Toro Negro
The island's highest peak, with trails surrounded by dense vegetation (see p90).

10 Cerro de Punta
A steep hike leading to the summit of Puerto Rico's highest peak (see p90).

For information about tours in Puerto Rico **See p110.**

Left **A parasailer at Playa Ocean Park** Center **Picnic area on Blue Beach** Right **Playa de Jobos**

Top 10 Beaches

Playa Ocean Park
Fronting the upscale neighborhood of Ocean Park *(see pp12–13)*, this is the preferred beach for the city's youth, who gather here on weekends to mingle and party. Beach volleyball is popular, as is parasailing *(see p36)*. Many of the area's middle-class mansions have now been turned into guesthouses for beach-loving vacationers. ◈ *Map X1*

Playa Isla Verde
This beach, to the east of Condado and Ocean Park, was named "Green Island Beach" for an uninhabited isle just offshore. Lined with trendy hotels, casinos, restaurants, and nightclubs, it is the most glamorous beach in San Juan. El San Juan Hotel & Casino *(see p114)* here is a destination in its own right *(see p62)*.

Green Beach
At the western extreme of Vieques, this lovely beach offers fabulous views across the Pasaje de Vieques to the main island. Snorkeling is superb in the shallow water, but avoid the northern end, which has strong currents. Avoid the beach entirely around dusk, when thousands of no-see-ums *(see p109)* are prevalent *(see p17)*.

Playa de Jobos
This dazzling beach, west of Isabela, is hemmed by limestone headlands that channel the Atlantic waves onto the shore. Several modest hotels and simple seafood restaurants cater to surfers here. The eastern headland has a blowhole – El Pozo de Jacinto – and is a spectacular vantage point for watching surfers, but be cautious when stepping over the jagged rocks. ◈ *Map C1*

Blue Beach
For four decades, this sensational beach on the south coast of Vieques was used by the US Navy for amphibious assault training. Curving around Bahía de la Chiva (Goat Bay), the lovely stretch of sand is backed by sea-grapes and cooled by strong winds that can pump high surf ashore at the west end. The rest of the bay is usually calm and good for kayaking. The waters around Isla Chiva, just offshore, offer fabulous snorkeling *(see p17)*.

Serene Green Beach

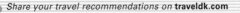

Playa Flamenco

6 This beach, which stretches for more than a mile (2 km), is considered to be the most beautiful in Puerto Rico. Its pure-white sands melt into vivid blue waters that are good for surfing on windy days. It has campsites, bathrooms, and picnic

Playa Flamenco, with its clear turquoise water

facilities under shade trees. World War II Sherman tanks, once used for target practice, stud the sands. The beach is a mere 2-minute taxi ride from the airport or 5 minutes from the ferry dock (see p18).

Playa Barrero

7 Brightly colored fishing boats are often drawn up on the sands of Playa Barrero, where fishermen repair their nets beneath trees. In winter, whales can often be seen close to the shore. Playa Barrero's west-facing position makes it one of the best places on the island from which to enjoy fiery sunsets. Map A3

Playa Dorado

8 This beach is named for its golden sands, most of which are taken up by resorts, such as the colorful Embassy Suites Dorado del Mar (see p116). The palm-shaded sands extend west to the popular Balneario Cerro Gordo beach (see p70), which has bathrooms and showers. Map H2

Playa El Combate

9 This beach can get crowded with Puerto Rican families on weekends and public holidays, when many arrive on speedboats and jetskis, but the beach is long enough that you can escape the crowds. Salt pans (salinas) inland offer excellent bird-watching if you tire of the beach (see p78).

Playa Piñones

10 Only a few miles east of the capital, this sweeping stretch of golden coastline can be reached by a walking and cycling track – a quicker route than the traffic-clogged coastal road on weekends. Food shacks on the beach serve interesting dishes such as fried yucca stuffed with crab, and watersports are available (see p95).

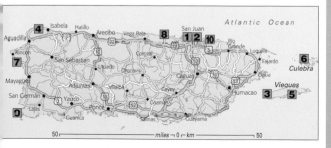

For exciting beach activities See pp36–7.

Left *Vejigantes* at Loíza Carnaval Right A Casals Festival performance

🔟 Festivals and Holidays

1 Ventana al Jazz
On the last Sunday of each month, La Ventana al Mar in Condado *(see p13)* becomes a venue for jazz music thanks to these concerts. Bring your own chairs, blankets, and refreshments. ◈ *Last Sun of month*

2 San Sebastián Street Festival
Puerto Ricans dressed in multi-horned devil masks and colorful costumes take to the streets for this exuberant parade in Old San Juan. After dusk, musicians perform and DJs spin merengue and salsa tunes, turning the streets into a riot of sound and motion. ◈ *Jan; dates vary*

3 Puerto Rico Heineken Jazz Festival
This week-long festival is one of the Caribbean's top jazz events and attracts thousands of visitors and locals alike, as Puerto Rican and big-name international jazz artists perform at various venues in San Juan. ◈ *May–Jun*

4 Casals Festival
Noted cellist Pablo Casals *(see p34)* founded this festival in 1957 to bring the world's best performers and guest conductors to Puerto Rico. Performances are usually hosted at the Centro de Bellas Artes Luis A. Ferré. ◈ *Feb–Mar • www.festcasalspr.gobierno.pr*

5 Fiesta de Reyes
"Three Kings' Day" commemorates the day the three wise men brought gifts to the baby Jesus. It rounds off the Christmas and New Year festivities and is a present-giving event – the governor of San Juan hands out gifts to children at his home on La Fortaleza street. ◈ *Jan 6*

6 Fiestas Patronales
Every town celebrates its own patron saint festival with religious processions, live music, parades, beauty contests, and often *topes* – displays of horsemanship. A *fiesta patronal* occurs somewhere on the island every week.

7 Loíza Carnaval
Puerto Rico's liveliest annual folk and religious ceremony honors Loíza's patron saint, John *(Santiago)* the Apostle, as well

Musicians performing at a *fiesta patronal*

Preceding pages **Stunning aerial view of Culebra**

as the town's African heritage, with processions featuring masked figures called *vejigantes* and *bomba* dancers performing to an Afro-Caribbean rhythm. ◈ *Late Jul*

8 Carnaval Ponceño
Many Puerto Rican towns organize some sort of carnival in the last week of February, but Ponce has the island's liveliest one. *Vejigantes* parade around, hitting people with *vejigas* (brightly painted balloons or dried pigs' bladders), while merrymakers enjoy live music and revelry in the streets. ◈ *End of Feb*

Carnaval Ponceño performers

9 Eugenio María de Hostos Day
The birthdate of the 19th-century educator, philosopher, and nationalist Eugenio María de Hostos is a national holiday. Families flock to the beach to relax and party. The town of Mayagüez, his birthplace, has a special ceremony. ◈ *2nd Mon of Jan*

10 Puerto Rico Discovery Day
Puerto Ricans commemorate the "discovery" of Borinquén in 1493 by Christopher Columbus on "El Dia de Descubrimiento." Parties take place on all of Puerto Rico's beaches at this time. ◈ *Nov 19*

Top 10 Local Customs

1 Politeness
Old-fashioned Hispanic courtesy is important, especially greeting people with formalities when introduced or entering a room.

2 Dress
Scruffiness is not appreciated. Even less well-to-do locals make an effort to dress as smartly as possible.

3 Hurrying
Not a Puerto Rican trait, and locals appreciate foreigners who know how to relax.

4 Machismo
Totally ingrained among local men, who like to flirt but expect their own women to be demure *(see p103)*.

5 Jokes
Puerto Ricans like to joke and also often make fun of unusual physical traits, but rarely with malice.

6 The Church
A large majority of Puerto Ricans are Catholic, although few attend church regularly.

7 Siestas
Elderly people and country folk like an afternoon nap, although offices and businesses stay open all day.

8 Politics
Party rivalry is keen and partisan positions are sharply defended. Avoid raising the issue of independence.

9 Punctuality
While buses, ferries, and tours normally leave on time, punctuality is less important at social gatherings.

10 Santeria
The majority of Puerto Ricans put their faith in saints to whom they pray, even if they don't always admit it.

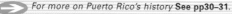 *For more on Puerto Rico's history* See pp30–31.

Left **Luis A. Ferré Science Park** Right **A rusting Sherman tank at Playa Flamenco**

🔟 Children's Attractions

1 Castillo de San Cristóbal

With its cannons, eerie tunnels, and museum of antique weaponry and military costumes, this castle makes history come alive. Guided tours put the past in perspective, and occasional re-enactments add thrilling drama (see pp10–11).

2 Parque de las Cavernas del Río Camuy

Children will enjoy identifying make-believe figures in the dripstone formations here, and spotting blind fish and blue-eyed crabs in the underground river. The massive cave system is also home to millions of bats. A trolley ride makes for a fun beginning and end to the tour (see pp20–21).

3 Museo del Niño

Housed in a colonial mansion in Old San Juan, this museum will keep children enthralled for hours with its interactive educational displays, which include NASA Space Place and exhibits on subjects ranging from human biology to hurricanes.
🔗 Map U6 • Calle Cristo 150, San Juan • 787 722 3791 • Open 9am–3:30pm Tue–Thu, 9am–5pm Fri, 12:30–5pm Sat–Sun • Adm • www.museodelninopr.org

4 Luis Muñoz Marín Park

Youngsters will love this huge forested and landscaped park, which has lakes with pedal-boats, as well as swings, slides, and Jungle Gyms. Bicycles and two- and four-seater cycles can be rented to roam the park, and there's also a miniature steam train. Jump on the cable car for great aerial views of the park.
🔗 Map T2 • Av Jesú Piñero, Hato Rey, San Juan • 787 763 0787 • Open 8:30am–5pm Wed–Sun

5 Arecibo Lighthouse and Historical Park

This theme park was built around the Neo-Classical Faro de los Morrillos lighthouse, which is now a maritime museum. The park has a mini-zoo, replica Spanish galleons and pirate's ship, a replica Taíno village, a pirate's cave, a salt-water aquarium, and a playground. The lighthouse is a great observatory for whale-watching in winter (see p70).

Arecibo Lighthouse and Historical Park's play area

6 Moisty Skate & Family Park

This popular venue is a nirvana for kids and a fun place for adults too. Attractions include skate parks, swimming pools, water slides and fountains. Other activities on offer are go-karting, paintballing, pony rides, and more. ⓢ Map K3 • Av Garrido, Caguas • 787 903 0504 • Open 10am–6pm Sun–Wed, 0am midnight Thu Sat • Adm • http://moisty.info/site

7 Luis A. Ferré Science Park

The Luis A. Ferré Science Park is San Juan's most extensive facility for families. It offers wide-ranging amusements that include a small zoo, military aircraft, seven themed museums, and a planetarium. You can also rent a pedal-boat for some family fun at the park's man-made lake (see p62).

8 Playa Flamenco

This spectacular beach on Culebra has lots of space for kids to run free. There are calm sections of shallow water which are ideal for wading, although it is always wise to supervise children while in the ocean. Marine turtles can sometimes be seen laying eggs here, and World War II Sherman tanks, rusting in the sand, make for an interesting opportunity to teach children about history (see p18).

A hippopotamus at Dr. Juan A. Rivera Zoo

9 Dr. Juan A. Rivera Zoo

This well-run zoo, the largest in Puerto Rico, is home to African wildlife, including lions, elephants, and gorillas. It also has Bengal tigers and a wealth of butterflies, while parrots and other tropical birds flit around in a large bird enclosure. Kids can hop aboard camels for rides on weekends (see pp74–5).

10 Coquí Water Park

The thrilling water park at El Conquistador Resort (see p116) makes a splash with its lazy river, winding tube slides, and vertical drop slides. A rope bridge, rapids, and waterfalls add to the drama, and there's a special section for very young children. ⓢ Map N2 • El Conquistador Resort, Fajardo • 787 863 1000 • Adm

Left *Santos* at Puerto Rican Arts & Crafts Center *Plaza Las Américas* Right *Mundillo lace slippers*

🔟 Places to Shop

1 Plaza Las Américas
The largest shopping complex in Puerto Rico has more than 200 shops, including well-known names such as Macy's and Banana Republic. Independent shops sell everything from cigars and jewelry to electronics. ✪ *Map T2 • Av FD Roosevelt 525, Las Américas Expressway, Hato Rey • 787 767 5202*

2 Moca
The traditional center of *mundillo* lace-making in Puerto Rico, Moca is the best place to buy beautiful blouses and table-cloths. You can see these being handmade on *telares* (lap boxes) at family-run crafts stores that open out on to the street. November is the best time to visit, when the *mundillo* festival is held. ✪ *Map B2*

3 Calle Fortaleza
This cobbled street in the heart of Old San Juan is lined with art galleries, boutiques, and craft stores. It gets crowded with shoppers when cruise ships are in port, so don't expect great bargains. Barrachina's *(see p63)* serves free rum as you peruse its arts and crafts, cigars, and jewelry. ✪ *Map U6 • Old San Juan*

A shop at Calle Fortaleza

4 Puerto Rican Arts & Crafts
This store has a huge selection of crafts, including a tremendous range of *santos* and papier-mâché carnival masks. A separate section sells gourmet Puerto Rican food items, while an art gallery at the rear sells exquisite silk-screened serigraphs. ✪ *Map U6 • Calle Fortaleza 204, Old San Juan • 787 725 5596*

5 La Calle
This is the best place in San Juan to buy irresistibly grotesque carnival masks *(caretas)*, made of papier-mâché and painted in gaudy colors. Prices range from $10 to $2,500, depending on quality and complexity *(see p63)*.

6 Plaza del Mercado de Santurce
Providing a taste of traditional Puerto Rico in the heart of the modern city, this atmospheric market (known as "La Placita") is a great place to haggle over fresh fruit and vegetables, handicrafts, and home-made remedies at *botánicas* (medicinal stalls). The vendors host street parties with live music and dancing on Thursday, Friday, and Saturday nights *(see p63)*.

An artist at work at Calle del Cristo

7 Calle del Cristo
This charming colonial street has many of Old San Juan's most stylish boutiques, as well as art galleries and lively cafés. Browse through paintings set out by artists on Plazuela Las Monjas, or pick up some creative and eclectic art and jewelry at Bóveda *(see p61)*.

8 Orocovis
Carved wooden *santos*, priced from $50 to $1,500, are the specialty of the artisans in this town. Most notable are the works of Celestino Avilés and his son Antonio Avilés Burgos. A good time to buy is during the Festival de Artesanías in September. ◈ *Map G4*

9 Avenida Ashford
This tourist strip is famous for its cosmopolitan shops and high-end boutiques selling quality ware. It also has lots of bars, cafés, restaurants, and day spas where you can relax after a day's shopping *(see p12)*.

10 Isla Verde Mall
This giant mall is perfect for visitors staying in the ritzy beachfront hotels, and offers great deals on clothes and jewelry, as well as on goods at its specialty stores, which range from pharmacies to a dive shop. ◈ *Map J2 • Av Isla Verde & Av Gobernadores, Carolina, San Juan • 787 748 0150*

Top 10 Souvenirs

1 Carnival Masks
These frightening papiermâché demon masks *(caretas)* make great wall-hangings. The best come from Ponce.

2 Coffee
Puerto Rico's mountain-grown coffee, hard to find off the island, can be bought at local specialty shops.

3 "Maboiti" Birds
These life-size bird figurines, hand-carved by Elpidio Collazo González (1937–2007), are now collectors' items.

4 Santos
These folksy hand-carved figures of Catholic saints are the quintessential Puerto Rican craft item.

5 Mundillo Lace
Delicate lace clothing and cloths handmade in Moca are eagerly sought by collectors.

6 Jewelry
San Juan is a great place to buy designer watches and jewelry at duty-free prices.

7 Music DVDs
There is a vast choice of merengue and salsa albums. Look for traditional *jíbaro* country music too.

8 Taíno-Inspired Ceramics
Well-crafted replicas of artifacts unearthed at Centro Ceremonial Indígena de Tibes *(see pp22–3)* can be bought in museums and craft stores.

9 Cigars
Hand-rolled Puerto Rican cigars are good value, as are Dominican imports, but Cuban cigars are not sold here.

10 Guayaberas
These tropical shirts for men are not only stylish, but also perfectly suited to the hot climate.

Left **Dragonfly** Right **A *lechonera* sign**

TOP 10 Restaurants

1 La Fonda del Jibarito
This family-run restaurant is an institution among locals, who flock for simple Puerto Rican fare, including specialties such as conch *ceviche* and chicken fricassee. ◈ Map V5
• Calle Sol 280, Old San Juan • 787 725 8375 • $$$

2 Casa Lola
Taste the best flavors from Puerto Rico's traditional cuisine, skillfully created by renowned chef Roberto Treviño, at this classy restaurant. Start with *empanadilla de ropa vieja* (Cuban beef stew empanadas) followed by skewers with pineapple and coconut fried rice (see p65).

A painting displayed at Barú

3 Lola
A fusion of taste and color, this popular eatery in Ponce offers gourmet cuisine that combines modern continental fare with Puerto Rican staples. Try the decadent fried cheescake (see p87).

4 Zest at The Water Club
At this beautiful restaurant treat yourself to an avant-garde culinary experience set in an amazing sub-aquatic atmosphere. Its modern Latin cuisine menu features

butter poached lobster tail, squid ink risotto with carrots beurblanc and crispy calamari (see p65).

5 Dragonfly
The Latin-Asian cuisine and sushi served at this San Juan restaurant come with creative twists. Ideally located in the heart of SoFo, the interiors of this upscale eatery resemble an old opium den in tropical Asia. Try the lobster mango summer rolls and tuna tartare on sushi rice tostones (see p65).

6 Horned Dorset Primavera
This restaurant is considered to be the finest in western Puerto Rico. Its nightly five-course fusion menu may include lobster in orange-flavored *beurre-blanc* sauce and pan-seared scallops (see p115).

Horned Dorset Primavera

For more restaurants See pp65, 71, 79, 87, 93, and 99.

ining room at Carambola

Carambola

7 This fine-dining restaurant
as the best Caribbean fusion
uisine on Vieques. Relax in its
tmospheric, candlelit dining
oom or enjoy the views from
:s romantic terrace *(see p99)*.

Lechoneras at Guavate

8 These simple, open-air
ateries *(see p112)* with outdoor
eating are a specialty of
Guavate. You're charged by the
veight of your plates. Live musi-
ians often perform. ◎ *Map K4
Junction of Carreteras 184 and 52,
Guavate • Open 11am–6pm Fri–Sun*

Beach Shacks,
Playa Piñones

9 Puerto Rican delicacies, such as
bacalaitos (codfish fritters), are
ried over open fires at wooden
iosks here. These are a great
ption for laid-back dining. A
hilled beer makes the perfect
ccompaniment. ◎ *Map L2*

Tamboo Beside the Pointe

10 This beachfront restaurant
pecializes in fresh fish and
eafood, with a menu that
hanges according to the catch
f the day. Diners can enjoy
heir meal – and delicious pina
oladas – while watching surfers
1 action. ◎ *Map A3 • Carretera 413
m 4.4, Marías Beach, Rincón • 787
23 8550 • $$*

Top 10 Bars

1 El Patio de Sam
A live-music bar selling
26 types of beer and excellent
hamburgers *(see p64)*.

2 Mist
A chic rooftop drinking
hole with a skyline swimming
pool and a live DJ *(see p64)*.

3 Small Bar
A trendy bar in Condada
area serving a wide variety of
artisan beers *(see p64)*.

4 La Taverna del Lupulo
This bar offers a huge
selection of beers and a rock-
ing nightlife. ◎ *Map U5 • Calle
del Sol 200, San Juan • 787 721
3772 • Open 3pm–1am Mon–Thu
(until 2am Fri & Sat, midnight Sun)*

5 Calypso Café & Bar
A great place for wraps,
sandwiches, and Saturday
brunch. ◎ *Map A3 • Carretera
413, Marías Beach, Rincón • 787
823 1626 • Open 11am–10pm*

6 Colmados
Grocery stores that often
double as working-class bars
(see p112).

7 La Terraza
Popular with Ponce's hip
young crowd – serves late-
night munchies *(see p87)*.

**8 Carli's Fine Bistro &
Piano**
Known for live jazz, martinis,
and gourmet cuisine. ◎ *Map
V6 • Calle Tetuán 206, San Juan
• 787 725 4927 • Open 11:30am–
3pm & 5–11:30pm Mon–Sat*

9 Bar Mar Azul
A bar with pool tables,
darts, and a juke box. ◎ *Map P4
• Isabel Segunda, Vieques • 787
741 3400 • Open 11pm–1am
Sun–Thu, 11pm–2:30am Fri–Sat*

**10 Plaza del Mercado
de Santurce**
A street party fueled by the
market vendors *(see p46)*.

Puerto Rico's Top 10

→ *For price ranges See p65.*

Left **Bistec encebollado** Right **Almejas casinos**

Puerto Rican Dishes

Piñon
A form of vegetable and ground beef casserole, *piñon de amarillos* contains no fewer than a dozen vegetables, herbs, and spices, including garlic. A key ingredient is fried plantain, layered with meat, shredded cheese, and scrambled egg. It is baked and broiled, and served with white rice.

Mofongo
A plantain-based favorite, *mofongo* is considered the national dish. Plantains are fried, mashed, and mixed with olive oil, crushed garlic, and sometimes pieces of bacon, and served as breakfast, or as a side dish. This creation can also be served stuffed with shrimp, but tastes just as good on its own.

Salmorejo
Originating in southern Spain, *salmorejo* is a thick crabmeat stew made with chopped and sautéed onions,

Salmorejo

peppers, and olives. It is usually served with fried plantains or *amarillos* – stewed green bananas, and is often sold at beachside kiosks.

Lechón a la Barra
Like most Latins, Puerto Ricans are crazy about pork, especially when it is fresh off the spit and served, still sizzling, with white rice, red beans, and fried plantain. This local delicacy is normally reserved for holidays and celebrations, but is also a weekend favorite, when whole pigs are slowly roasted over charcoal fires.

Mofongo with shrimp

Bistec Encebollado
Puerto Ricans put their own twist on beefsteak with onions. The steak is prepared with a vinegar and garlic "rub," and then smothered in caramelized onions. It can be served with any type of rice. Green salad and *tostones (see sidebar)* make a good accompaniment too.

Mondongo
Not to be confused with *mofongo*, this is a formidable dish comprising cow's (and sometimes pig's) stomach (tripe) diced and slowly stewed in a tomato and garlic sauce. It is a popular dish for Sunday brunches – Puerto Ricans believe that it can help cure a hangover.

Arroz con gandules

7 Arroz Con Gandules
Rice with pigeon peas is a staple of any special occasion in Puerto Rico, and has many variations. This dish is usually seasoned with *sofrito* – an aromatic mix of herbs and spices – and diced ham. A dash of tomato sauce helps impart a lovely flavor.

8 Serenata de Bacalao
This original Puerto Rican dish – saltcod salad – is eaten as an appetizer or light lunch. Flakes of faintly salted cod are tossed in a light vinaigrette with sliced onions, potatoes, and other vegetables, and then laid on a bed of lettuce and garnished with hard-boiled egg and olives.

9 Tembleque
No wedding, child's birthday party, or other special event would be complete without this rich, creamy coconut pudding. It quivers like jelly, hence the name *tembleque*, which means "jiggling." The delicious dessert resembles a custard and is served topped with cinnamon.

10 Almejas Casinos
A Puerto Rican seafood favorite, baked stuffed clams are found on many restaurant menus. The freshly caught clams are prepared in their shells and garnished with parsley, bacon, butter, and dry white wine. They are then baked and served with hot clam juice.

Top 10 Puerto Rican Snacks

1 Tostones
A side dish of unripe plantains that are fried, pounded flat, and then refried.

2 Alcapurrias
A mixture of ground plantain and *yautía* filled with crab meat or ground beef and deep fried.

3 Bacalaitos
Fried fritters made with a mix of cod, garlic, cilantro, and other seasonings.

4 Almojábanas
Delicious cheese-flavored rice fritters deep-fried and sometimes served with hot chocolate or avocado sauce.

5 Arañita
Shredded and deep-fried plantains usually eaten with garlic sauce. These look like spider legs, hence the name "little spiders."

6 Pasteles
Fold-over pasties made of various types of dough, yuca, or plantain filled with ground meat, diced meat, or vegetables, and then fried

7 Sorrullitos
Fried cornmeal fritters traditionally stuffed with cheese and sometimes dusted with powdered sugar.

8 Setas
Mushrooms are never more popular than when sautéed with garlic, olive oil, white wine, and parsley.

9 Batatas
Boiled or roasted yam (sweet potatoes) served with butter, garlic, and parsley

10 Papas Rellenas
Mashed and fried potato balls stuffed with seasoned beef – these make a very popular side dish.

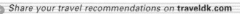
*Share your travel recommendations on **traveldk.com***

Mangrove-lined lagoon

🔟 Trees and Flowers

1 Royal Palms

The stately *palma real* towers 82 ft (25 m) and has a silvery trunk that is slightly bulbous at the top. Its fronds are used for thatch, its seeds are used as pig feed, and the soft and succulent palm heart from the center of the trunk is a delicacy used in salads.

2 Sierra Palms

The "mountain palm" is indigenous to the region and lives above an elevation of 1,640 ft (500 m). Its exposed buttress roots, similar to those of mangroves, are an unusual feature that help the sierra palm cling to steep terrain and unstable soil.

3 Coconut Palms

The undisputed symbol of the Caribbean is the slender coconut palm, which thrives in moist, sandy soils and is found all along Puerto Rico's shores. Native to Asia, it was introduced to the Americas in 1542. Virtually every part of the coconut palm is used by humans, including the large nut with its delicious meat and refreshing juice.

A pink poinsettia

4 Poinsettias

Originally indigenous to Mexico, these perennial flowering shrubs, known as *pascuas*, are popular during Christmas because of their flame-red and green leaves, although they can also be white or pink.

5 Mangroves

Five species of mangroves *(manglares)* thrive along the island's shores, forming tangled forests that trap sediment and prevent coastal erosion. Their stilt roots rise above the water, forming labyrinthine creeks that are vital nurseries for marine life.

6 Jacarandas

Remarkable for their springtime flowering, when purple-blue blossoms burst forth, with a peak in April, jacarandas are often used to brighten up Puerto Rico's urban parks and highway medians. The trees' prized timber is coveted by carpenters.

Coconut palms on the coast

A sprig of orchids

7 Orchids

Puerto Rico boasts hundreds of species of orchids, including many endemics. These plants are renowned for their exquisite flowers, and many wild orchid species are endangered by illegal collecting. The San Juan Orchid Society holds a Festival de Orquídeas each March. ◈ *San Juan Orchid Society • 787 758 9981*

8 Gumbo-Limbos

A hardy species with huge branches, gumbo-limbos are also known as "naked Indian trees"– their reddish-brown, paper-thin bark peels off in sheets like sunburnt skin. These trees readily sprout from branches stuck into the ground.

9 Ceibas

Sacred to the Taíno, silk-cotton trees grow to 230 ft (70 m) and have straight, branchless trunks studded with spines. Buttress roots help to stabilize these massive trees, the branches of which form wide canopies.

10 Epiphytes

These plants take root on the branches of other trees. Many species, such as Spanish moss, put down hanging roots, while some, like bromeliads, gather water in cisterns formed by tightly overlapping leaves.

Top 10 Fruits

1 Guanábana

Also called soursop, this fruit makes a slightly sour, creamy drink when juiced.

2 Papaya

This tear-shaped fruit has delicious yellow flesh. Its seeds are used as a folk remedy for intestinal parasites.

3 Mamey

A melon-like fruit with a yam-like flavor, mamey is mainly used for ice creams and *batidas* (milkshakes).

4 Custard Apple

The moderately sweet flesh of this fruit is used to make a popular drink with medicinal properties.

5 Guayava

This small fruit has slightly acidic flesh and many small, hard seeds. It is commonly used in jellies or as a dessert with cheese.

6 Tamarind

This tree's pendulous fruit is too tart to eat. The pulp is often used to make juice.

7 Passion Fruit

This golf-ball sized fruit is known as *parcha* – its yellow flesh is tart and makes a delicious topping for desserts.

8 Banana

Known worldwide, this curved fruit with yellow skin has cream-colored flesh loaded with vitamins, making for a healthy snack.

9 Breadfruit

This fruit can grow as large as a basketball. Its flesh is cooked and mashed, often with coconut milk.

10 Mango

Mangoes have highly fragrant, pulpy, and slightly fibrous flesh that is deliciously sweet and juicy.

Left **Mona iguana** Right **Leatherback turtle**

Animal Life

1 Leatherback Turtles

These are the largest of the five marine turtle species that nest on Puerto Rican beaches, notably on Vieques and Culebra. Unlike other turtles, which have internal skeletons, leatherbacks have bony plates covered with an external leathery skin. They feed mainly on jellyfish.

2 Sapo Conchos

These endemic toads have a long, curved snout and horned protuberances above the eyes. Once widespread, they are now restricted to the Bosque Estatal de Guánica *(see p83)* and are threatened with extinction, partly due to competition from the toxic marine toad, introduced to the island in the 19th century to control insects.

3 Manatees

Manatees are gentle marine mammals resembling a tuskless walrus, and weigh up to half a ton (500 kg). They propel themselves with a spatulate tail and feed on aquatic vegetation. The West Indian manatee is endangered – many are killed by collisions with speedboats.

4 Ponce Anoles

These bright-green, tree-dwelling lizards are nicknamed *lagarjito gigantes* (giant lizards). Like all anoles, they mark their territory by extending a fan-like dewlap beneath the neck and by bobbing up and down. Keep an eye out for ponce anoles performing this comic behavior on tree trunks.

5 Coquís

These thimble-sized frogs are the nation's unofficial mascots. Inhabiting various ecosystems, from coastal dry forest to rain-soaked El Yunque, they are more often heard than seen, thanks to their nocturnal two-note cheep – "ko-KEE".

6 Dolphins

Several species of these endearing, sociable, and highly intelligent marine mammals swim in the ocean waters surrounding Puerto Rico. They often accompany passing boats, such as the Fajardo-Vieques ferry *(see p98)*, and are popular in marine parks, where many are trained to perform amazing acrobatics.

Manatee

Puerto Rican Boas

7 These endangered, non-venomous snakes, endemic to the island, can grow to 9 ft (3 m). They are found mostly in the karst region of Puerto Rico, where they feed on bats. In sunlight, their skin gives off an iridescent blue sheen.

Humpback Whales

8 The Mona Passage, which separates Puerto Rico and Hispaniola, is a migratory path for these marine mammals, which can grow to a staggering 50 ft (15 m). It is enthralling to see a humpback leap clear out of the ocean (see p110).

Humpback whale

Bats

9 Puerto Rico has 13 species of bats, which represent 80 per-cent of the island's mammal species. Most live in caves and emerge at night to feed on mosquitoes, fruit, and nectar; the bulldog bat also catches fish.

Mona Iguanas

10 This species of iguana is found only on Isla Mona (see p75) and can reach 3 ft (1 m) in length. Despite their dragon-like appearance, mona iguanas are harmless vegetarians. They bask in the sun to become active and live on very sparse vegetation.

Top 10 Birds

Cattle Egrets

1 These heron-like, snow-white birds can be seen in almost any field, especially around flea-ridden cattle.

Yellow Warblers

2 Nicknamed "mangrove canaries," these mangrove dwellers are excellent singers.

Lizard Cuckoos

3 Listen for the tell-tale guttural laugh of these tawny endemics, which are identified by their red eye-rings.

Emerald Hummingbirds

4 The *zumbadorcito*, the world's second-smallest bird, was once worshipped by the Taíno as a "god bird."

Puerto Rican Parrots

5 The island's green endemic parrots are critically endangered and fewer than 50 remain in the wild.

Puerto Rican Woodpeckers

6 These woodpeckers, found throughout the island, can be heard using their sharp beaks to drill holes in tree trunks.

Puerto Rican Screech Owls

7 These small birds, nicknamed "coo-coos" for their call, can often be heard at dawn.

Red-Billed Tropicbirds

8 These graceful, snow-white seabirds have a long, forked streamer tail and a pin-sharp red bill.

Frigatebirds

9 Black birds with a massive wing-span, frigatebirds roost atop mangroves and steal from other seabirds.

Pelicans

10 These birds, identified by their long beak with a pouch, skim the ocean surface.

AROUND
PUERTO RICO

PUERTO RICO'S TOP 10

Left **Condado beach** Center **Statue at Plaza de San José** Right **Cannon balls at Castillo de San Cristóbal**

San Juan

FROM THE ATMOSPHERIC CHARM OF THE OLD CITY *to the sophistication of Condado and Isla Verde, San Juan is a lively city that mixes history with contemporary chic. Old San Juan is a lived-in museum of colonial cobbled streets and plazas replete with cathedrals, convents, and colorful mansions, many of which are now boutique hotels, restaurants, and bars. Gorgeous beaches just a few minutes away are lined with luxurious resort hotels and casinos. The city's museums, theaters, art galleries, and lively festivals satisfy the most demanding of culture enthusiasts.*

10 Sights

1. Old San Juan
2. Condado
3. Castillo de San Cristóbal
4. Paseo de la Princesa
5. Plaza del Inmigrante
6. Fortaleza San Felipe del Morro
7. Plazuela de la Rogativa
8. Museo de Arte de Puerto Rico
9. Calle del Cristo
10. Plaza de San José

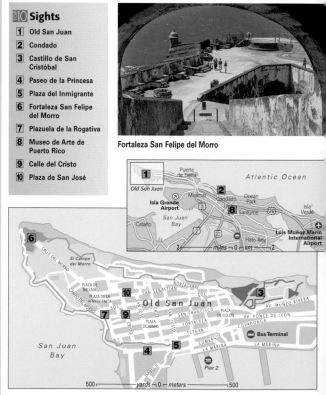

Fortaleza San Felipe del Morro

Preceding pages **Sculpture on the Raíces Fountain on Paseo de la Princesa**

A cruise ship anchored at Old San Juan

Castillo de San Cristóbal

This imposing bastion dominates the eastern approach to the city and was intended to guard against invasion by land. Cannons sit proudly atop the ramparts, pointing toward the ghosts of pirates past. Restoration work has added to its majesty, and the barracks have been turned into a museum showing how they would have looked in colonial times. Free guided tours help bring the past to life (see pp10–11).

Old San Juan

There's a good reason more cruise ships anchor at Old San Juan than at any other port in the Caribbean – this charming quarter has something for everyone. Steeped in history, Old San Juan is packed with interesting things to see, from its quaint, cobbled streets overhung with wooden balconies to its massive fortresses and ancient city walls. The National Historic Zone has more than 900 buildings of historic importance, as well as tiny plazas with bohemian cafés and stylish bars that burst into life at night (see pp8–9).

Condado

East of Old San Juan, the Condado district is reminiscent of Miami's South Beach, not least for its Art Deco buildings. Beautiful beaches that stretch for 3 miles (5 km) are a very popular venue for locals, especially on holidays and weekends. Avenida Ashford runs parallel to the shore and is lined with gleaming, high-rise condominiums and upscale hotels needling the sky. The boulevard also teems with chic, modern fashion outlets, cosmopolitan restaurants, lively casinos, and sophisticated nightclubs that exemplify the city's cool, sophisticated Latin vibe (see pp12–13).

Paseo de la Princesa

Leading west from Plaza del Inmigrante, this pedestrian-only promenade, lit by antique street lamps, is ideal for an evening stroll. It ends at the base of Fortaleza San Felipe del Morro, where waves crash against the seawall. Stop to admire the Raíces Fountain, which celebrates the island's multicultural heritage. Musical performances are held here on Sundays, and stalls are set up on weekends (see p9).

Raíces Fountain at Paseo de la Princesa

Plaza del Inmigrante

5 Also known as Plaza de la Marina because it opens onto the cruise port, this sloping cobbled plaza was built in the 19th century and boasts several impressive buildings. Soaring over the north side is the Banco Popular, a graceful Art Deco structure built in 1939 and adorned with faces of ancient gods. On the east side, the stately Antiguo Edificio de Correos (post office) and Neo-Classical Edificio Federal (Federal Building) add stature to the tree-shaded square *(see p9)*.

Fortaleza San Felipe del Morro

6 Building work on this fortress began in 1539 and was completed in 1786. It was designed to guard the harbor entrance and connected to Castillo de San Cristóbal by massive walls. Today a National Historic Monument restored and maintained by the US National Parks Service, it displays colonial weaponry and uniforms in the former barracks, and cannons can be admired in their embrasures. A lighthouse, built here in 1843, offers fine vistas over the Campo del Morro, a swathe of greenery separating the fortress from the heart of Old San Juan *(see p8)*.

Plazuela de la Rogativa's statue

Plazuela de la Rogativa

7 This tiny square offers excellent views over Paseo de la Princesa and the harbor, and is a good place to take photographs at sunset. Its focal point is a statue of a bishop and three women bearing lit torches, which commemorates a night in 1797 when the local bishop led a torch-lit procession that fooled an invading English fleet into believing that Spanish reinforcements had arrived. ⊗ Map T6

Museo de Arte de Puerto Rico

8 This vast museum, housed partly in a former hospital and partly in a modernist wing, is one of the largest art galleries in the Caribbean, with 1,100 works on display. It exhibits Puerto Rican art, from 16th century religious works to contemporary masterpieces. Be sure to explore the sculpture garden

A gallery at the Museo de Arte de Puerto Rico

The blue-tiled Calle del Cristo

outside. ◈ Map T1 • Av José de Diego 299, Santurce • 787 977 6277 • Open 10am–5pm Tue & Thu–Sat, 10am–8pm Wed, 11am–6pm Sun • Adm

9 Calle del Cristo

The pretty Calle del Cristo is paved with blue-tiled cobblestones and lined with charming two-story townhouses graced by wooden balustrades that today double as art galleries, boutiques, and cafés. The Catedral de San Juan Bautista (see p9), the city's ecclesiastical 1852 masterpiece, presents a striking facade. The street ends at the tiny Capilla del Cristo (Christ Chapel). ◈ Map U5–6

10 Plaza de San José

With its neatly clipped trees and quaint colonial buildings, this ancient plaza is one of Old San Juan's most delightful areas. At its center stands a life-size statue of Ponce de León. Other sights in the vicinity include the Museo Pablo Casals (see p62) and the Iglesia San José, famous for its muraled ceiling. Calle San Sebastián's bars and restaurants have a great atmosphere, especially at night (see p9).

A Morning Walk Around Old San Juan

Early Morning

After a hearty breakfast, head to **Plaza del Inmigrante**. Admire the buildings surrounding the square and then walk west along **Paseo de la Princesa**, pausing to photograph the **Raíces Fountain**. If it's a weekend, then browse the arts and crafts stalls set up here. Passing through the **Puerta de San Juan**, the old city gate, turn left for **Plazuela de la Rogativa**, and admire the fine view toward the harbor. Follow Calle Las Monjas east one block to view the **Catedral de San Juan Baútista** (see p9) before following cobbled Calle del Cristo uphill to **Plaza de San José**. Just around the corner is the **Museo Pablo Casals** (see p62), dedicated to the world-famous cellist. Stop to take a coffee break at one of the plaza's many cafés and indulge in some leisurely people-watching.

Mid-Morning

Refreshed, trace your steps back to **Parque de Beneficencia** and turn left. The huge Neo-Classical building ahead houses the **Instituto de Cultura Puertorriqueña** (see p9). Call in to see its eclectic exhibits, including fascinating pre-Columbian artifacts, before continuing north across the wide open Calle del Morro to the **Fortaleza San Felipe del Morro**. This massive fortress will take the better part of an hour to explore before the airy stroll back to the **Plaza de San José** area for lunch.

Left **Bacardi Rum Distillery** Center **Luis A. Ferré Science Park** Right **Town hall at Plaza de Armas**

🔟 Best of the Rest

1 Instituto de Cultura Puertorriqueña
This cultural institute has peaceful courtyards and displays of Taíno artifacts, religious icons, and contemporary art *(see p9)*.

2 Plaza de Armas
A former military parade ground, Plaza de Armas is surrounded by exquisite buildings in elegant styles. It is a social gathering spot by day *(see p9)*.

3 Bacardi Rum Distillery
Guided tours of the world's largest rum factory end with a demonstration on mixing cocktails. 🖎 *Map K2 • Carretera 888 Km 2.6, Cataño • 787 788 8400 • Open 9am–6pm Mon–Sat, 10am–5pm Sun*

4 Catedral de San Juan Baútista
This 19th-century Neo-Classical structure features lovely ceiling frescoes and a marble mausoleum containing the remains of Ponce de León *(see p9)*.

5 Playa Isla Verde
The main draws of this beach are its deluxe hotels, casinos, and nightclubs, especially the El San Juan Hotel & Casino *(see p114)*. 🖎 *Map U2*

6 Luis A. Ferré Science Park
This park has a zoo, museums, a planetarium, and a lake with boats. 🖎 *Map K2 • Carretera 167, Bayamón • 787 740 6868 • Open 9am–4pm Wed–Fri, 10am–6pm Sat–Sun • Adm*

7 Museo Pablo Casals
This small museum is full of memorabilia exploring the life of Spanish cellist Pablo Casals *(see p34)*. 🖎 *Map U5 • Calle San Sebastián 101, San Juan • 787 723 9185 • Open 9:30am–4:30pm Tue–Sat • Adm*

8 Puerta de Tierra
This former buffer zone between Old San Juan and Condado has some fine buildings, such as the Neo-Classical El Capitolio (Capital Building) and the Art Deco Normandie Hotel *(see p114)*, which resembles an ocean liner. 🖎 *Map S1 • Capitolio: Av Muñoz Rivera; 787 721 6040; open 9am–4pm Mon–Fri; guided tours by appointment*

9 Parque de las Palomas
This small plaza, named for the pigeons that flock here, overlooks Paseo de la Princesa and San Juan harbor. Sit on one of the benches to take in the view. 🖎 *Map U6 • Calle del Cristo*

10 Hotel El Convento
A fine hotel that was once a convent and later a brothel, El Convento has a good restaurant and rooftop bar *(see p114)*.

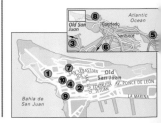

Left **Panama hats at Olé** Center **An emerald necklace from Emerald Isles** Right **La Calle**

Places to Shop

1 Barrachina's
Not only is this a great place for jewelry, cigars, and perfume, but it also has a patio bar serving piña coladas, which are said to have been invented here. ◎ *Map U6 • Calle Fortaleza 104 • 787 752 7912*

2 Bóveda
This long and narrow store houses an eclectic array of jewelry, hats, sunglasses, and clothing. A local favorite. ◎ *Map U6 • Calle del Cristo 209 • 787 725 0263*

3 Emerald Isles
Artisanal jewelry at reasonable rates make this a favorite with cruise passengers seeking emeralds or reproductions of pre-Colombian jewelry. ◎ *Map U6 • Calle Fortaleza 105 • 787 977 3769*

4 La Calle
This is a great place to look for colorful Puerto Rican carnival masks, from simple designs to quality collector pieces. It also displays fine works of art. ◎ *Map U6 • Calle Fortaleza 105 • 787 725 1306*

5 Club Jibarito
The store stocks branded luxury watches and jewelry, as well as high-quality Puerto Rican cigars. ◎ *Map U6 • Calle del Cristo 202 • 787 724 7797*

6 Linen House
Pick up baby clothes and tablecloths here, made with exquisite *mundillo* lace. ◎ *Map U6 • Calle Fortaleza 250 • 787 721 4219*

7 Plaza del Mercado de Santurce
With dozens of stalls and stores, this lively market is a great place to browse for trinkets and traditional medicines. ◎ *Map W2 • Calle Dos Hermanos & Calle Capitol, Santurce • 787 723 8022*

8 Olé
If you are seeking an authentic Panama hat to ward off the sun or look stylish, this store delivers. It also sells *santos (see p47)* and an eclectic array of Latin American crafts. ◎ *Map U6 • Calle Fortaleza 105 • 787 724 2445*

9 Spicy Caribbee
This is an excellent place to pick up local condiments, such as spicy sauces, fruit preserves, and hard-to-find gourmet Puerto Rican coffee. ◎ *Map U6 • Calle del Cristo 154 • 787 725 7259*

10 Mercado de Río Piedras
Locals flock here to buy fresh produce, CDs, and local fashions, such as men's *guayaberas* (colorful shirts). ◎ *Map X2 • Paseo de José de Diego • 787 763 3438 • Open 9am–5:30pm Mon–Sat, 9am–noon Sun*

Left **Blue Bar at El San Juan Resort & Casino** Right **Entrance to the trendy Parrot Club**

Nightlife

1 Small Bar
Small in size but huge on variety, this cool little bar offers a large selection of craft beers and international music. ⊗ *Map V1 • Av Ashford, San Juan • 787 402 2954 • Adm*

2 Club Brava
Stylish locals line up to enter this chic lounge-disco, where DJs spin a mix of Latin and international sounds. ⊗ *Map U2 • El San Juan Hotel, Av Isla Verde 6063 • 787 791 2781 • Open 10pm–3am Thu–Sat • Adm*

3 Blue Bar
Drawing a mix of young and old, this lobby bar buzzes on Saturday nights. ⊗ *Map U2 • El San Juan Resort & Casino, Av Isla Verde 6063 • 787 791 1000 • Open 6pm–3am*

4 Mist
Relax on leather loungers at this rooftop bar, which serves fancy cocktails, plays world music, and has sensational views. ⊗ *Map U2 • Water & Beach Club Hotel, 2 Tartak St • 787 728 3666 • Open 7–1am Mon–Thu, 7–3am Fri & Sat*

5 Parrot Club
Kick up your heels to live Latin jazz and salsa at this atmospheric bistro-restaurant. ⊗ *Map V6 • Calle Fortaleza 636 • 787 725 7370 • Open 6pm–midnight*

6 Luis A. Ferré Performing Arts Center
Also known as Bellas Artes, this complex boasts four theaters and hosts everything from stand-up comedy to ballet. The Puerto Rico Symphony Orchestra performs in the 1,880-plus capacity Festival Hall. ⊗ *Map T1 • Av Ponce de León, Santurce • 787 724 4747 • Adm*

7 Oceano
Sophistication and glamor characterize this magical place that offers a wide range of cocktails. ⊗ *Map W1 • 2 Vendig St, Condado • 787 724 6300 • Open noon–midnight Tue, Wed & Sun (until 2am Thu, 3am Fri & Sat)*

8 Nuyorican Cafe
Salsa lovers must visit this exciting venue for its sizzling hot live music. ⊗ *Map V6 • San Francisco St 312, San Juan • 787 977 1276 • Open 7pm–late daily*

9 Krash Klub
This gay club has dance floors on two levels and plays disco tunes. ⊗ *Map T1 • Av Ponce de León 1257, Santurce • 787 722 1131 • Open 10pm–3am Wed–Sun • Adm*

10 El Patio de Sam
This popular café-bar often plays live music. ⊗ *Map U5 • Calle San Sebastián 102 • 787 723 1149 • Open 11am–11pm Sun–Thu, 11am–2am Fri–Sat*

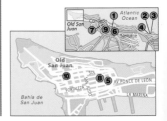

Price Categories

For a three-course meal for one with half a bottle of wine (or equivalent meal), taxes, and extra charges.

$	under $10
$$	$10–$20
$$$	$20–$30
$$$$	$30–$40
$$$$$	over $40

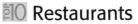

Pikayo's minimalist interior

TOP 10 Restaurants

1 Aguaviva
Check out the stylish lights at this restaurant, which serves creative dishes, such as the *torre del mar* (tower of seafood). ◎ Map W6 • Calle La Fortaleza 364 • 787 722 0665 • Open 11am–4pm • $$$$$

2 Casa Lola
Experience some of the best flavors of Criollo cuisine at this restaurant, which is housed in a plantation-style mansion. ◎ Map T1 • Av Ashford 1006, Condado • 787 998 2918 • Open 11:30–1am daily • $$$$$

3 Lemongrass
Dine on Pan-Asian Latino food indoors or on a patio overlooking ponds. There is also a sushi bar here. ◎ Map T1 • Caribe Hilton Hotel, Condado • 787 721 0303 • Open 6:30–10:30pm Mon–Sat • $$$$

4 Zest at The Water Club
Uniquely decorated to give the venue a submarine feel, this hip restaurant serves Puerto Rican fare with creative twists. ◎ Map U2 • Calle Tartak 2, Isla Verde • 787 728 3666 • Open 6–10pm Tue–Sat • $$$$$

5 Parrot Club
This trendy bistro's *nouvelle* Puerto Rican cuisine and live jazz draw elite crowds *(see p64)*. ◎ Map V6 • Open 11am–4pm & 6pm–midnight • $$$$$

6 Pamela's Caribbean Cuisine
This restaurant serves healthy Caribbean dishes, such as salads, with style. You can dine here with your toes in the sand. ◎ Map T1 • Calle Santa Ana 1, Ocean Park • 787 726 5010 • Open noon–3pm & 7–10:30pm • $$$$

7 Dragonfly
This is the city's most talked about restaurant for great Latin-Asian food and interesting drinks. ◎ Map V6 • Calle Fortaleza 364 • 787 977 3886 • Open 6pm–late daily • $$$$$

8 Trois Cents Onze
This French bistro has lovely Andalusian tilework and a good wine list. ◎ Map V6 • Calle Fortaleza 311 • 787 725 7959 • Open noon–3pm & 6:30–10:30pm Tue–Thu, noon–3pm & 6:30–1:30pm Fri–Sat, 5–10pm Sun • $$$$$

9 Palio
Try the huge Angus beef porterhouse steak here. ◎ Map V6 • Sheraton Old San Juan Hotel & Casino, Calle Brumbaugh 100 • 787 721 5100 • Open noon–4pm & 5–11pm • $$$$

10 Pikayo
Enjoy gourmet Creole cuisine in a chic, minimalist setting. ◎ Map V1 • Conrad Condado Plaza Hotel, 999 Ashford Ave, Condado • 787 721 6194 • Open 6–11pm • $$$$$

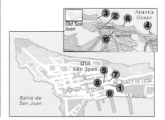

Left **Playa de Jobos** Center **Sculpture at Plaza de la Revolución, Lares** Right **A fountain in Arecibo**

North Coast

WEST OF SAN JUAN, THE ISLAND'S *palm-studded north shore is lined with glorious beaches,* the most beautiful of which are found around Dorado. Scenic mountains that have been eroded into a dramatic karst landscape of rugged gorges, spectacular caves, and sculpted rock formations called mogotes rise inland from the narrow coastal plain. This rugged scenery is at its finest around the Arecibo Observatory – the world's largest radio telescope – and nearby Parque de las Cavernas del Río Camuy. Several forest preserves tempt hikers, and one of the nation's most impressive ceremonial sites can be explored at Caguana. The mountain drive to reach it leads through several villages renowned for arts and crafts.

Arecibo Observatory's reflector and apparatus

🔟 Sights

1. Parque de las Cavernas del Río Camuy
2. Dorado
3. Arecibo Observatory
4. Arecibo
5. Karst Country
6. Parque Ceremonial Indígena Caguana
7. Playa de Jobos
8. Bosque Estatal de Guajataca
9. Lares
10. Bosque Estatal Cambalache

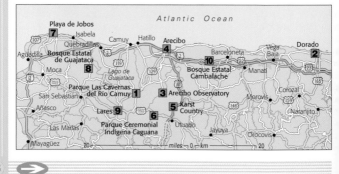

Stalactites at Parque de las Cavernas del Río Camuy

Arecibo Observatory

Resembling a James Bond movie set (in fact, it appeared in *GoldenEye*), the world's largest radio telescope comprises a 1,000-ft- (305-m-) wide spherical bowl made of 40,000 perforated aluminium panels and suspended across a huge limestone sinkhole. A triangular platform hanging 1,300 ft (400 m) above the dish houses receivers that monitor emissions, such as radio waves, from the earth's outer atmosphere to sources at the outer limits of the universe. The Angel Ramos Foundation Visitor Center provides audio-visual displays and interactive exhibits on the observatory, and on atmospheric and space sciences in general. ◎ *Map F2*
• *Carretera 625 Final* • *787 878 2612*
• *Open 9am–4pm (closed Mon & Tue Jan 16–May 31 & Aug 1–Dec 14)* • *Adm*
• *www.naic.edu*

Parque de las Cavernas del Río Camuy

The third-largest cave system in the world, this vast underground complex consists of hundreds of caverns. Fascinating guided tours begin and end with a tram ride and lead through the largest cave of all, which is full of weird and wonderful dripstone formations. Paths run alongside an underground river to the base of an enormous sinkhole. Visitors come away with an appreciation of the natural processes that have shaped this rugged region *(see pp20–21)*.

Dorado

This town is best known for its golden beaches lined with palm trees – remnants of a former coconut plantation. The town's Hyatt Hacienda del Mar boasts some of the best stretches of beach, and golfers can tee off at the resort's three championship golf courses. The main square, Plaza de Recreo, has a monument honoring the island's ethnic diversity.
◎ *Map J2* • *Hyatt Hacienda del Mar: Carretera 693 Km 12.8; 787 796 3000; www.hyatthaciendadelmar.hyatt.com*

Monument celebrating Dorado's ethnic heritage

Arecibo

Founded in 1616, this large coastal town is today a major manufacturing center that retains many wooden colonial structures, notably on Calle Alejandro Salicrup. The delightful Plaza Luis Muñoz Rivera is worth visiting for its 19th-century Neo-Classical cathedral and city hall, but most intriguing is the Logia Tanamá, a grandiose Romanesque building that serves as a Masonic hall and is fronted by an impressive bronze statue of a leaping dolphin. ◎ *Map E2*

Karst Country

5 Covering a sixth of the island, this distinctive landscape of sheer-sided *mogotes* (rock formations) and plunging canyons is the remnant of a great limestone plateau that rose from the sea in the Jurassic era and has since been worn away by water. The region is stippled with free-standing formations rising 985 ft (300 m) or more, and riddled with caverns and sinkholes. ◈ *Map E3*

Parque Ceremonial Indígena Caguana

6 A great starting point for learning about the island's indigenous culture, Caguana was one of the most important Taíno ceremonial sites in the Caribbean. The site, which was first excavated in 1915, features 12 *bateyes* (ancient ball courts) walled by slabs etched with petroglyphs, including the *Mujer de Caguana* – a female fertility figure with legs outspread. Taíno ceramics and other artifacts are displayed in a tiny museum here. ◈ *Map E3* • *Carretera 111 Km 12.3, Utuado* • *787 894 7325* • *Open 8:30am–4:20pm* • *Adm*

Playa de Jobos

7 Prime surf washes ashore at this windswept beach favored by surfers. Its laid-back appeal is enhanced by its many simple seafood restaurants and bars. You can watch surfers pass by the rugged limestone headland, Punta Jacinto, where spray blasts from a blowhole. The snorkeling is good in sheltered coves, and horseback rides on the beach add further thrills. ◈ *Map C1*

Bosque Estatal de Guajataca

8 This 6-sq mile (15-sq km) preserve is laced with close to 28 miles (44 km) of trails that weave through karst terrain. Before you begin your hike, pick up a map at the ranger station, from where a short trail leads to a *mirador* (lookout tower). Follow the more challenging 8-mile (13-km) Sendero Cabralla to Lago de Guajataca, a peaceful

Bateye at Parque Ceremonial Indígena Caguana

Plaza de la Revolución, Lares

reservoir where you can rent a boat and fish for bass. ⊗ *Map C2 • Carretera 446 Km 10, Guajataca • 787 872 1045 • Open 8am–5pm*

9 Lares

The scenic drive to reach Lares is reason enough to visit this small mountain town, which is famous for El Grito de Lares (The Cry of Lares), the nationalist uprising that launched the island's independence movement. A 19th-century cathedral stands over Plaza de la Revolución, but the square's most popular building is the Heladería de Lares, where you can buy tropical fruit-flavored ice creams. ⊗ *Map D3 • Heladería de Lares: Calle Lecaroz, Lares; 787 897 3290*

10 Bosque Estatal Cambalache

This forest preserve is ideal for hiking and mountain biking with just 4 miles (6 km) of level trails among royal palms, teak, and trees endemic to the island, such as *matabuey*. The karst scenery is spectacular, with trails winding along canyon bottoms at the base of soaring *mogotes*. Bird-watchers can spot endemic species such as the Puerto Rican bullfinch. Bats are numerous and swarm out of their caves at sun-set. ⊗ *Map F2 • Carretera 682 Km 6.6 787 881 1004 • Open 9am–4pm*

A Drive Through Karst Country

Morning

🕐 Begin your drive at the coastal town of **Arecibo**. After exploring the city's main sites, head south along Carretera 129, and then follow the signs that lead uphill to the **Arecibo Observatory**. After two hours of exploring the visitor center and admiring the radio telescope and the spectacular setting here, drive down south toward the **Parque Ceremonial Indígena Caguana**. About one hour is required to explore this fascinating Taíno cere-monial site. Then follow Carretera 111 west to the charming mountain town of **Lares** where you can have lunch. Try the tropical fruit-flavored ice cream at **Heladería de Lares**.

Afternoon

Continue your drive northward on Carretera 129 for **Parque de Las Cavernas del Río Camuy**, where you can take a guided excursion into the caverns; it can be cool, and the walkways are slippery, so carry along a sweater and wear shoes with good grip. Then press on westward on Carretera 119 for **Lago de Guajataca**, a man-made lake, and the **Bosque Estatal de Guajataca** – you can stop here for a short hike or fish for bass. Don't forget to keep an eye on the road as you take in the wonder-ful karst scenery along Carretera 113. Pass through the town of **Quebradillas** and continue northwest to **Playa de Jobos**. This beach is a good place to surf. You can also sample some local cuisine at **Happy Belly's** *(see p71)*.

Left **Día de los Santos Inocentes** Center **Playa Crash Boat** Right **Arecibo Lighthouse & Historical Par**

🔟 Best of the Rest

1 Día de los Santos Inocentes
Held every year since 1823 in Hatillo, the "Day of the Holy Innocents" features locals in fancy costumes and masks.
🇸 *Map D1 • Dec 28*

2 Hacienda Esperanza
This sugar estate displays old steam machinery and is surrounded by a wildlife refuge.
🇸 *Map F2 • Carretera 616 Km 4 • 787 722 5844 • Guided tours by appointment • www.fidecomiso.org*

3 Arecibo Lighthouse and Historical Park
Children will love this beachfront facility, with its playground, mini-zoo, aquarium, and "Pirate Boardwalk." 🇸 *Map E2 • Carretera 655, Arecibo • 787 880 7540 • Open 9am–6pm Mon–Fri, 10am–7pm Sat–Sun • Adm • www.arecibolighthouse.com*

4 Punta Borinquen
The beaches here offer excellent scuba diving, and there is a golf course. 🇸 *Map B1 • Punta Borinquen Golf and Country Club: Carretera 107, Ramey Base, Aguadilla; 787 890 2897*

5 Isla Desecheo
The coral reefs and underwater grottoes surrounding this uninhabited island are very popular dive sites. 🇸 *Map B1*

6 Isabela
Famous for lace production, this small town hosts the Festival del Tejido (Lace Festival) each May. 🇸 *Map C1*

7 Playa Crash Boat
This popular surfers' beach, which is used by local fishermen is named for the rescue boats that set out to save Ramey Air Force Base pilots who came down at sea. 🇸 *Map B2*

8 Reserva Natural Laguna Tortuguero
Spot migratory waterfowl, endemic birds, and caimans – small reptiles – at this coastal wetland preserve. A visitors' center has interesting wildlife exhibits. 🇸 *Map G2 • Carretera 687 Km 1.2 • Open 6am–5pm Wed–Sun*

9 Balneario Cerro Gordo
Run by the local municipality, this popular beach has showers, bathrooms, and shacks serving good food. It gets lively on weekends and holidays when Puerto Rican families flock here. 🇸 *Map H1*

10 La Cueva del Indio
The Indian Cave, which has been hewn out of coastal cliffs, displays superb examples of Taíno petroglyphs. Don't miss the natural bridge formation nearby. Wear sturdy shoes for the craggy limestone underfoot. 🇸 *Map E1 • Carretera 681 Km 7.8*

Price Categories

For a three-course meal for one with half a bottle of wine (or equivalent meal), taxes, and extra charges.

$	under $10
$$	$10–$20
$$$	$20–$30
$$$$	$30–$40
$$$$$	over $40

El Ladrillo's interesting interiors

🔟 Restaurants and Bars

1 La Villa Dorada de Alberto
Situated on the beachfront, this lively eatery serves superb seafood in a great atmosphere. ✪ Map H2 • Calle E #99 Urb Costa De Oro, Dorado • 707 278 1715 • Open 11am–9pm Sun–Thu, 11am–11pm Fri–Sat • $$$

2 Pollos Chano
This local favorite may appear completely outdated, but it serves the best *pollo asado* (roast chicken) on the west side of the island. ✪ Map B2 • Camino Agustín Stall & Calle Fuerte, Aguadilla • 787 891 4866 • Open noon–8pm • $

3 El Ladrillo
Brick walls decorated with artworks add ambience to this traditional steakhouse, which also serves high-quality seafood. ✪ Map H2 • Méndez Vigo 334, Dorado • 787 796 2120 • Open 11:30am–3pm & 6–10:30pm Tue–Sun • $$

4 Cocina Creativa
Tuck into the Jamaican jerk chicken, fish cakes, gourmet coffees, smoothies, and cheesecake that feature on this delightful café's eclectic menu. ✪ Map B2 • Carretera 110 Km 9.2, Aguadilla • 787 890 1861 • Open 9am–5pm • $$

5 Salitre
A nautically themed beachfront restaurant, Salitre offers seafood dishes, such as shrimp cocktail and the fresh catch of the day. ✪ Map E2 • Carretera 681 Km 3.8, Arecibo • 787 816 2020 • Open 11am–9pm Sun–Thu, 11am–11pm Fri–Sat • $$$

6 Restaurant Histórico El Puente Blanco
This ocean-facing restaurant serves Italian fare, as well as seafood and local dishes, including *mofongo (see p50)*. ✪ Map D2 • Carretera 4484 Km 1.9, Quebradillas • 787 895 1934 • Open 11:30am–11pm • $$$$

7 Happy Belly's
Plenty of American and local favorites, including burgers and *mofongo*, are served at this laid-back restaurant by the beach. ✪ Map C1 • Carretera 466 Km 7.5, Playa de Jobos • 787 872 6566 • Open 10am–11pm Sun–Tue, noon–3am Wed–Sat • $$

8 El Buen Café
Dine at the lively café or the air-conditioned restaurant, both of which sit across from Parador El Buen Café Hotel *(see p117)*. Try the *carne mechada* (stuffed pot roast) served here. ✪ Map D1 • Carretera 2 Km 84, Carrizales, Hatillo • 787 897 1000 • Open 5:30am–10pm • $$$

9 Olas y Arenas
The home-made gourmet dishes at this airy restaurant features fresh herbs from its very own garden. ✪ Map C1 • Carretera 466 Km 8.9, Playa Montones, Isabela • 787 872 2045 • Open 7am–10pm • $$

10 Ocean Front Bar & Grill
Savor creative Caribbean cuisine at this elegant restaurant and bar on the beach. ✪ Map C1 • Carretera 400, Playa de Jobos • 787 872 3339 • Open 11am–10pm Mon–Thu (until midnight Fri–Sun) • $$$$

Recommend your favorite restaurant or bar on **traveldk.com**

Left **Elephant at Dr. Juan A. Rivero Zoo** Center **Cabo Rojo beach** Right **Museo de Aguada**

West Coast

THIS WILD AND DRAMATIC REGION BOASTS *some of the most beautiful coastal scenery in Puerto Rico. To the north lies Rincón, a resort town known for its stunning sunsets, excellent whale-watching during winter, and world-class surfing. Uninhabited and rugged Isla Mona is a wildlife refuge*

surrounded by coral reefs that draw divers, while bird-watchers flock to Boquerón Bird Refuge and the salt flats around Cabo Rojo. The village of La Parguera offers exciting boat trips to Bahía de Fosforescente, named for its bioluminescent waters. Moca, which lies inland, is a center for traditional lace production, Mayagüez has a fine plaza and zoo, and the town of San Germán draws visitors keen on colonial architectural gems.

Iglesia de San Germán de Auxerre

🔟 Sights

1. San Germán
2. Rincón
3. Aguada
4. Plaza Colón, Mayagüez
5. Horned Dorset Primavera
6. Moca
7. Whale-Watching
8. Dr. Juan A. Rivero Zoo
9. Isla Mona
10. Cabo Rojo

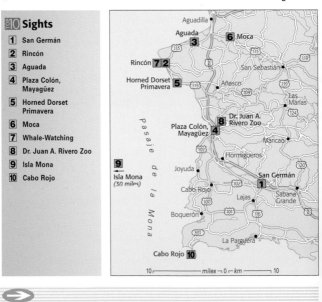

1 San Germán

Puerto Rico's second-oldest town, the "City of the Hills" dates from 1573, although most of its lovely colonial buildings were built during the 19th-century coffee boom *(see p90)*. The quaint plazas and narrow streets that make up the historic center are lined with ornate mansions and centuries-old churches, including the Iglesia Porta Coeli, which houses the island's pre-eminent religious museum. The town comes to life every July with its *fiesta patronal (see p42)* – a festival honoring its patron saint *(see pp24–5)*.

2 Rincón

This resort town occupies a triangular peninsula facing the Mona Passage. It is a great base in summer for snorkeling and diving, and in winter for whale-watching. Rincón is home to some of the Caribbean's best surf breaks, and boasts great beaches, from wave-washed Playa María to reef-protected Playa Barrero *(see p39)*, where colorful fishing boats line the sands. Accommodations range from simple campsites to chic boutique hotels, including the stately Hotel Horned Dorset Primavera *(see p115)*; lively beach bars and eateries provide great perches from which to enjoy the sunsets. ◔ *Map B3*

3 Aguada

This historic town is claimed by locals to be the site where Christopher Columbus stepped ashore in

Lighthouse at Rincón

1493, although the residents of Aguadilla *(see p78)* make a similar claim. In the center is the Iglesia San Francisco de Asís, with its lovely stained-glass windows, and the former train station, which is now home to the Museo de Aguada, an impressive history museum. If possible, time your visit for mid-November, when locals parade to honor Columbus' arrival. ◔ *Map B2 • Museo de Aguada: Av Nativo Alers 7; 787 868 6300; open 8am–noon & 1–4pm Mon–Fri*

4 Plaza Colón, Mayagüez

A large square in the center of Puerto Rico's third-largest city, Plaza Colón is adorned with a magnificent Neo-Classical town hall and a clock tower, a large statue of Christopher Columbus, and various other bronze statues. Locals gather to play dominoes in the shade of jacaranda trees that burst into purple bloom in spring. The Teatro Yagüez, a block north, is worth a visit for its Neo-Classical pillars and Art Nouveau windows and dome. ◔ *Map B4 • Teatro Yagüez: Calle McKinley; 787 833 5195; open 8am–4:30pm; guided tours by appointment*

Plaza Colón's town hall

The elegant Horned Dorset Primavera

5 Horned Dorset Primavera

This hacienda-style hotel, which is part of the prestigious Relais & Chateaux chain and is named for a species of English sheep, stands over its own small beach at Rincón. You don't have to stay in the luxurious accommodations here to enjoy the seafront restaurant, which serves gourmet cuisine and has a formal dress code. Visitors can also sign up for a yoga class in the open-air pavilion *(see p115)*.

6 Moca

Moca is known as the center of *mundillo* lace production

Monument to the Lace Weaver, Moca

in Puerto Rico, where it is still made in a traditional manner at family workshops *(see pp46–7)*. The Museo del Mundillo explores this popular, centuries-old art form. The town hosts the Mundillo Festival each June and the main plaza honors the tradition with a Monument to the Lace Weaver. ◈ *Map B2*
• *Museo del Mundillo: Calle Barbosa 237, 787 877 3815; open 9am–1:30pm Tue–Fri, 9am–4pm Sat; adm; www.museodel mundillo.org*

7 Whale-Watching

Humpback whales pass through the Mona Passage from December to March en route to and from warm-water mating and calving zones. Whale-watching trips depart Rincón *(see p110)*, but the giant marine mammals can also be seen from shore. You can use the giant binoculars at El Faro lighthouse, where whales are often seen within 660 ft (200 m) of shore. There are few wildlife experiences as thrilling as this. ◈ *Map A3* • *El Faro: Area Recreativa del Faro, Rincón; open 8am–4pm*

8 Dr. Juan A. Rivero Zoo

This spacious, imaginatively landscaped zoo delights visitors with its collection of more than 300 species of animals and birds from throughout the tropics. Elephants, rhinos, and zebras wander a safari park here, while lions, leopards, and Bengal tigers prowl their own arenas. An enclosure for chimpanzees,

Humpback Whales

These marine mammals can grow to 50 ft (15 m) long and weigh up to 40 tons. Virtually the entire population of 12,000 North Atlantic residents migrate to warm Caribbean waters during the winter to mate and give birth. Humpbacks frequently "breach," or throw their bodies out of the water and splash down on their backs. Males also sing during the mating season; the complex songs change every year. In summer, the creatures return north to feed on krill and small fish.

a children's park, and camel rides help keep kids enthralled.
⊗ Map B4 • Carretera 108, Mayagüez • 787 834 6330, 787 834 8110 • Open 8:30am–5pm Wed–Sun • Adm

Isla Mona

This uninhabited isle a few miles west of the main island is fringed by soaring cliffs. The wildlife refuge protects the nesting sites of boobies, tropic-birds, and other seabirds, as well as marine turtles. Iguanas crawl the sun baked surface of the island, which is studded with cacti and riddled with caves. One of two trails leads past a former mine, and you can camp overnight with a permit. The crystal-clear waters and coral reefs guarantee good diving. Hire a boat in Rincón for the 2-hour trip here. ⊗ Map A4

Cabo Rojo

"Red Cape," named for its reddish cliffs, is topped by a hexagonal Neo-Classical light-house, Faro Los Morrillos, built here in 1881. The wave-battered cape shelters a rocky, white sand beach that is backed by marshy salt flats offering great bird-watching opportunities. It is advisable to stay away from the unstable clifftops. ⊗ Map B6

Faro Los Morrillos, Cabo Rojo

A Walk Around San Germán

Early Morning

Half a day is enough to see the main sights of this historically significant town. Begin on the east side of **Plaza Santo Domingo** (see p24) with a trip to the Spanish-mission style **Iglesia Porta Coeli** (see p24). View the fascinating collection of carved wooden saints in the religious art museum housed here. Afterwards, admire some of the restored 19th-century gingerbread-style mansions in the streets around the plaza and on nearby Calle Dr. Santiago Veve and Calle Ramos. A highlight is **Casa Morales** (see p25), a quintessential Victorian design, on the northeast corner of the plaza.

Mid-Morning

Back in the plaza, walk west along Calle Ruiz Belvis to **Plaza Francisco Mariano Quiñones** (see p25), passing the alcaldía (town hall) en route. The tree-shaded plaza is graced with wrought-iron lamp posts and has benches where you can relax, study the park's topiary bushes, and take in the local life. Enter the **Iglesia de San Germán de Auxerre** (see p25), which dates from 1739 – be sure to note the church's beautiful tromp l'oeil ceiling. Continue along Calle Dr. Santiago Veve to view the **Casa Lola Rodríguez de Tió** (see p25), home of patriot-poet Lola Rodríguez de Tió. After all the sightseeing, head to the popular **Mike's Steak House** (see p79) for its excellent chargrilled steaks and seafood, or to **Chaparritas** (see p79) for some Mexican fare.

Left **A wading bird at Boquerón Bird Refuge** Right **Marine turtle**

Wildlife-Viewing

1 Whale-Watching
The gargantuan humpback whales feed in the Northern Atlantic but migrate in winter to warm Caribbean waters to mate and give birth. February is the peak month for viewing them in the Mona Passage *(see p110)*.

2 Boquerón Bird Refuge
This coastal wetland, part of the Bosque Estatal de Boquerón, is a superb place for spotting migratory waterfowl, wading birds, and hawks. Blinds (covered areas to disguise bird-watchers) enhance your experience. ◉ *Map B6 • Carretera 301 Km 5.1, Boquerón • 787 851 7258 • Open 8am–4pm Tue–Sun*

3 Bahía Bioluminiscente
This lagoon, not to be confused with a bay of the same name off Vieques, glows due to the microscopic organisms that emit light when disturbed. Glass-bottomed boat trips depart La Parguera *(see next page)*.

4 Manatees
These huge vegetarian marine mammals *(see p54)* can be seen swimming in coastal lagoons around Boquerón and La Parguera. They are difficult to spot, so a sighting is a rare treat.

5 Mona Iguanas
The charcoal-brown Mona Iguana *(see p55)* is endemic to Isla Mona. This egg-laying reptile is easily spotted as you walk the island's trails.

6 Red-Footed Boobies
Isla Mona is a nesting site for red-footed boobies – large seabirds with salmon-colored feet. They nest on the ground and display relatively little fear of humans.

7 Marine Turtles
Several beaches on Isla Mona and Isla Magueyes are nesting sites for leatherback and other marine turtles *(see p54)*. These endangered creatures face numerous threats, including marine pollution.

8 Tropical Agricultural Research Station
This facility on the University of Puerto Rico's western campus occupies a former plantation. Self-guided trails lead through one of the world's largest tropical botanical gardens. ◉ *Map B4 • Av Pedro Albizu Campos 2200, Mayagüez • 787 831 3435 • Open 7am–noon & 1–5pm Mon–Fri*

9 Dolphins
These charming and playful marine mammals *(see p54)* are a joy to see. They accompany fast-moving boats, leaping in and out of waves at the bow.

10 Corals
The waters around Isla Desecheo *(see p70)* abound with colorful coral species, including brain corals, boulder corals, and 6-ft- (2-m-) tall sea fans. Sponges are a highlight here. ◉ *Map B1*

Left **Scuba diver encountering a jelly fish** Right **Playa El Combate**

TOP 10 Outdoor Activities

1 Surfing
Rincón is the perfect place for surfing, and its mix of breaks makes it ideal for beginners or experts. Several outfitters rent boards and offer lessons for all levels *(see p110)*.

2 Kayaking
Several hotels in Rincón, such as the Horned Dorset Primavera *(see p115)*, provide one- and two-person sea kayaks for paddling around reef-protected ocean waters. ◈ *Map A3*

3 Jogging at Rincón
Rincón's endlessly long beaches are ideal for casual runs, with the bonus of fantastic scenery and plenty of waterfront bars and restaurants along the way if you need to take a break *(see p73)*.

4 Scuba Diving
Isla Desecheo *(see p70)* is a favored spot for diving, although it requires an hour-long boat ride from Rincón. A B-29 bomber off Aguadilla is closer to shore and equally exciting *(see p110)*.

5 Hiking on Isla Mona
This island has two hiking trails, which are good for viewing mona iguanas, red-footed boobies, and frigatebirds up close, as well as century-old mining equipment. Visit some of the island's remote beaches between May and October to spot marine turtles nesting.

6 Bird-Watching at Las Salinas
The seasonal lagoons of the Las Salinas salt flats draw American oystercatchers and thousands of other waterfowl. There is a watch-tower that provides good views. ◈ *Map H5*

7 Strolling Playa El Combate
Stretching for several miles, this slender beach is a pleasure to walk along, but you'll want to avoid dusk when no-see-ums *(see p109)* are active. ◈ *Map B5*

8 Jet-Skiing at La Parguera
On weekends and holidays, locals flock to this coastal resort village, where jet-skis can be rented to buzz around the inshore lagoons. ◈ *Map C5–C6*

9 Swimming at Bahía Bioluminiscente
Take a kayak trip and swim at night in Bahía de Bioluminiscente for a surreal experience. You'll be amazed to see yourself glow with an eerie halo. ◈ *Map C5–C6*
• Paradise Scuba & Snorkeling Center
• 787 899 7611 • Adm • www.paradise scubasnorkelingpr.com

10 Snorkeling
Marine life is abundant amid the colorful coral reefs off La Parguera. The underwater world is easily seen while snorkeling in shallow water close to shore.
◈ *Map C5 • Paradise Scuba & Snorkeling Center • 787 899 7611 • Adm • www. paradisescubasnorkelingpr.com*

Left **Boats docked at La Parguera** Center **Aguadilla's plaza** Right **One of the beaches at Boquerón**

🔟 Best of the Rest

1 San Sebastián
This hill town is an important center of coffee production. The surrounding mountains feature *mogotes* (conical peaks) and a waterfall. ◈ *Map C3*

2 Hacienda El Jibarito
Learn about coffee production at this restored coffee *finca* (farm). Guided hikes and bird-watching excursions are also on offer. ◈ *Map C3 • Carretera 445 Km 6.5, San Sebastián • 787 280 4040 • www.haciendaeljibarito.com*

3 Corozo Salinas
Glistening mountains of salt and evaporating pools lie beside vast salt flats inland of Bahía Salinas. An educational center has displays. ◈ *Map E6 • Las Salinas • 787 254 0115 • Open 8am–5pm Mon–Fri*

4 Playa El Combate
This slender beach is named for a battle in 1759 between two communities that fought for rights to adjacent salt flats. It gets crowded on weekends and holidays. ◈ *Map B5*

5 Boquerón
A former fishing village, Boquerón today derives its income as a laid-back resort. Enjoy its two pleasant beaches and the many street stalls selling oysters – a local specialty. ◈ *Map B5*

6 Aguadilla
This town's gorgeous bay setting is best viewed from the seafront boulevard. A monument in Parque Colón stands where Christopher Columbus supposedly landed in 1493. ◈ *Map B2*

7 Bosque Estatal de Boquerón
This state preserve protects mangrove and dry tropical forest, and is replete with endemic wildlife. You can spot birds at the Boquerón Bird Refuge *(see p76)* or hire boats in La Parguera to explore the lagoons. ◈ *Map B6*

8 La Parguera
Set in a bay studded with mangrove-fringed cays, this bustling resort is popular for its bars and restaurants, and trips to Bahía de Bioluminiscente *(see p77)*. ◈ *Map C5*

9 Sabana Grande
This town, famous for its thatch-palm baskets and other goods, hosts the Petate Festival in December. The Sanctuary for the Virgin Mary here is a pilgrimage site. ◈ *Map C5*

10 Isla Magueyes
Boat trips from La Parguera drop you on this island, where iguanas are easily spotted. The dive sites here are frequented by sharks. ◈ *Map C6*

Price Categories

For a three-course meal for one with half a bottle of wine (or equivalent meal), taxes, and extra charges.	
$	under $10
$$	$10–$20
$$$	$20–$30
$$$$	$30–$40
$$$$$	over $40

Left **Agua al Cuello's seaside setting** Right **The family-run La Casita**

TOP 10 Restaurants

1 Agua al Cuello
Enjoy the sunset as you dig into the seafood and steaks served here. There is live music on Saturday nights and Sunday evenings. ◎ *Map B5 • Bahía Salinas Beach Resort & Spa, Carretera 301 Km 11.5, Boquerón • 787 254 1212 • Open noon–9pm • $$*

2 Las Cascadas
Set in a parador, this is a great breakfast spot; try the *omelet cascada*. The dinner menu includes *criolla* dishes and lobster. ◎ *Map B5 • Carretera 101, Boquerón • 787 851 2158 • Open 7:30–10:30am & 5–8pm daily • $$*

3 Chaparritas
This Mexican *cantina* serves tasty fare, including filling *burritos* and *enchiladas*, Tex-Mex snacks, and spicy shrimps in tequila. ◎ *Map C5 • Calle Luna 171, San Germán • 787 892 1078 • Open 11:30am–10pm Mon–Fri, 6–10pm Sat • $$*

4 Horned Dorset Primavera
Dine on gourmet French-inspired cuisine in a romantic and elegant setting inside this hotel. Reservations are required and a strict dress code applies *(see p115)*. ◎ *Open 7–10pm • $$$$$*

5 The English Rose
Enjoy stunning views of the sea and the tranquility of the hills, while having a leisurely breakfast or brunch at this lovely restaurant. ◎ *Map A3 • Carr. Interior 413, Km 2, Rincón • 787 823 4032 • Open 8am–noon • $$*

6 Pampas
Meats are grilled at your table at this steakhouse, which also serves local dishes. Enjoy the live music on weekends. ◎ *Map B4 • Av Hostos 351, Mayagüez • 787 831 0655 • Open 11am–10pm Mon–Sat, 11am–8pm Sun • $$$*

7 Mike's Steak House
A casual restaurant, Mike's Steak House is renowned for its quality chargrilled steaks. It also serves seafood. ◎ *Map C5 • Av Castro Pérez 132, San Germán • 787 892 3581 • Open 11am–10:30pm Mon–Sat, 11am–10pm Sun • $$*

8 El Castillo
This restaurant is known for its lunch buffets and international menu that features seafood and meat dishes with unusual sauces. ◎ *Map B4 • Carretera 104 Km 0.3, Mayagüez • 787 832 3030 • Open 6:30am–midnight • $$*

9 Las Brasas at Rincón Beach Resort
This Mediterranean-themed restaurant specializes in *nouvelle* Caribbean dishes and has a large wine selection. ◎ *Map A3 • Carretera 115 Km 5.8, Rincón • 787 589 9001 • Open noon–8pm (to 9pm Thu–Sat) • $$$*

10 La Casita
This simple, family-run restaurant with an open-air terrace is known for its Puerto Rican plates. ◎ *Map C5 • Carretera 304 Km 3.3, La Parguera • 787 899 1681 • Open 11am–10:30pm Tue–Sun • $*

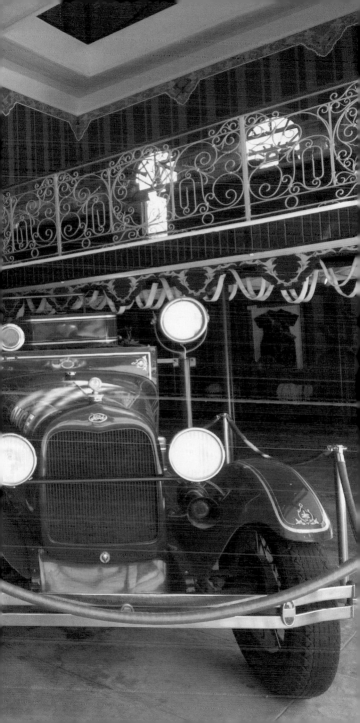

Left **An old fire truck at Museo Antiguo Parque de Bombas** Right **Museo Castillo Serrallés**

South Coast

FRAMED TO THE NORTH BY THE CORDILLERA CENTRAL, *the narrow and relatively dry southern coastal plain has only a few good beaches, but draws nature-lovers with its wildlife-rich Bosque Estatal de Guánica and Bahía de Jobos, a mangrove forest best explored on a kayak. Ponce, the island's second-largest city, delights with its restored historic core and world-class art museum. Divers marvel at The Wall – a dramatic coastal drop-off with dozens of excellent dive sites that teem with marine life. History fans are drawn to the indigenous ceremonial site at Tibes, the time-warp sugar-processing town of Aguirre, and antique coffee plantations such as Hacienda Buena Vista.*

🔟 Sights

1. Centro Ceremonial Indígena de Tibes
2. Museo de Arte de Ponce
3. Catedral de Nuestra Señora de la Guadalupe
4. Bosque Estatal de Guánica
5. Museo Antiguo Parque de Bombas
6. Hacienda Buena Vista
7. Museo Castillo Serrallés
8. The Wall
9. Gilligan's Island
10. Central Aguirre

Catedral de Nuestra Señora de la Guadalupe

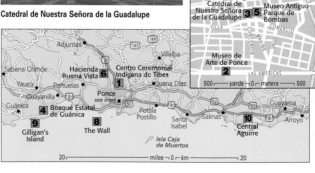

Preceding pages **An antique fire truck at Museo Antiguo Parque de Bombas**

Centro Ceremonial Indígena de Tibes

1 Centro Ceremonial Indígena de Tibes

This pre-Columbian site in the hills north of Ponce was only unearthed in 1975, when floodwaters revealed the Taíno ruins. Guides take visitors on tours that lead past 12 *bateyes* – ceremonial ball courts – as well as petroglyphs and an ancient cemetery. The site was inhabited by the Igneri, a pre-Taíno tribe, and artifacts of both cultures are exhibited in a museum here, which shows a 30-minute video and displays an adult skeleton in the fetal position *(see pp22–3)*.

2 Museo de Arte de Ponce

More than 3,000 works of art by European masters and well-known painters from North and South America, along with Puerto Rican art spanning three centuries, are displayed at this spectacular museum. Works by Rodin, Delacroix, Gainsborough, and Puerto Rico's foremost artists are among the permanent displays, but the museum is most famous for Lord Frederic Leighton's eye-catching *Flaming June (see pp26–7)*.

3 Catedral de Nuestra Señora de la Guadalupe

This grand cathedral, with its striking, twin-spired, Neo-Classical facade, was designed by architects Francisco Porrata Doría and Francisco Gardon in the 1930s and built on the site of a building that was destroyed in the 1918 earthquake. Rising over Plaza Las Delicias, the white and duck-egg-blue church honors the city's patron saint, the Virgin of Guadalupe. The interior boasts stained glass windows, a grandiose alabaster altar, and a huge pipe organ installed in 1934. ◈ *Map F5 • Plaza Las Delicias, Ponce • Open 6am–1:30pm Mon–Fri, 6am–noon & 3–8:30pm Sat–Sun*

4 Bosque Estatal de Guánica

Guánica State Forest protects acres of dry deciduous forest spanning the east and west shores of Bahía Guánica. Its mosaic of habitats comprises moist and shady ravines and exposed ridges, and the flora and fauna is replete with mangrove swamps. Spanish moss and mistletoe festoon tree branches, and agaves and cacti pierce the sun-baked soils. More than 100 bird species flit among the branches, nimble size frogs hop around underfoot, iguanas scurry about the leaf litter, and marine turtles lay their eggs in pristine sands. The forest has 36 miles (58 km) of trails. ◈ *Map D6*

Hiking at Bosque Estatal de Guánica

→

Ponce Massacre

Nationalist sentiment against US occupation boiled over on March 21, 1937 during a pro-independence rally in Ponce's Plaza Las Delicias. When the nationalists began singing the Puerto Rican national anthem, armed police opened fire, killing 17 civilians. Two policemen were also killed in the melee, now known as the Ponce Massacre.

5 Museo Antiguo Parque de Bombas

This photogenic Arabesque structure, on the east side of Plaza Las Delicias, served as the city's fire station for over a century. Now a museum, it hosts an antique fire truck and 19th-century hand-pulled water tanks. Other exhibits poignantly recall a fire in the US Army's artillery store in 1899 that threatened to destroy Ponce; the fire-fighters disobeyed orders to retreat and saved the city. ○ *Map F6 • Av Marina and Av Cristina, Plaza Las Delicias, Ponce • 787 284 3338 • Open 9am–5pm daily*

6 Hacienda Buena Vista

This coffee plantation in the hills north of Ponce dates from 1833 and features an original hydraulically operated processing mill, complete with giant water wheel and water-powered turbine. The former slave quarters, storage sheds, and the owner's house are all furnished with original 19th-century pieces. The gift shop sells coffee and preserves from fruit still grown here. ○ *Map F5 • Carretera 123 Km 16.8 • 787 722 5882 (Mon–Fri); 787 284 7020 (Sat–Sun) • Open Wed–Sun; guided tours by appointment • Adm • www.fideicomiso.org*

7 Museo Castillo Serrallés

This majestic Spanish Renaissance-style mansion stands atop El Vigía Hill, high above Ponce. It was built in the 1930s by the Serralles family, owners of the Don Q rum distillery. Guided tours lead through rooms filled with hand-carved period furnishings and paintings, and a permanent exhibit explores Puerto Rico's sugarcane and rum industries. The lush, landscaped gardens and courtyards offer panoramic vistas over Ponce. ○ *Map F5 • Calle Vigía 17 • 787 259 1774 • Open 9:30am–5:30pm Thu–Sun • Adm*

8 The Wall

The continental shelf along Puerto Rico's south coast plunges into an abyss that is like an underwater Grand Canyon. This drop-off – "The Wall" – extends along

The striking Museo Antiguo Parque de Bombas, Ponce

Boats anchored at Gilligan's Island

...22 miles (35 km) of coast between Ponce and La Parguera (see p78), and offers great diving. Beginning at a depth of just 50 ft (15 m), the steep drops and canyons, which are studded with coral formations, teem with marine life. ✆ Map C6–F6

9 Gilligan's Island

This uninhabited mangrove-ringed cay, named for its similarities to the island in the popular US sitcom Gilligan's Island, lies less than half-a-mile (1 km) offshore of Bosque Estatal de Guánica. It is rimmed with beaches that dissolve into turquoise shallows where conditions are perfect for snorkeling. Restrooms and picnic tables serve day-trippers, who flock here on weekends. ✆ Map D6

10 Central Aguirre

Built around the Central Aguirre Sindicate sugar refinery near Salinas in the late 19th century, this once-thriving company town had plantation-style houses, a theater, bowling alley, hotel, hospital, and even a golf course. The company closed in 1990 and the town has since been left to decay, but its ruins serve as a legacy of a once-glorious era. ✆ Map H6

Walk Around Ponce

Early Morning

🕐 Begin your half-day tour at **Plaza Las Delicias**, where you can admire the fountain and various statues, and explore the **Museo Antiguo Parque de Bombas** and **Catedral de Nuestra Señora de la Guadalupe**. Stroll around the plaza's perimeter to admire the 1847 townhall on the south side, and Romanesque 1899 **Casa Armstrong Proventud** on the west. Turn south along Calle Marina for the **Casa de la Masacre de Ponce** (see p86). This lovely colonial structure is now a museum honoring the 17 nationalists killed by police during the 1937 demonstration. Retrace your steps to Plaza Las Delicias and turn right onto Calle Cristina. Walk down a block to admire the imposing Neo-Classical **Teatro La Perla** (see p86), erected in 1941.

Mid-Morning

One block further east, turn left onto Calle Salud. Ahead, on the southeast corner of Calle Isabel, and peruse the **Museo de la Música Puertorriqueña** (see p86). This museum is housed in an exquisite Art Nouveau building and displays fine exhibits tracing Puerto Rican music through the centuries. Walk west along Calle Isabel to the **Museo de la História de Ponce** (see p86), which features a scale model of the city among its historical exhibits. Continue to walk west along Calle Isabel to the Ramada Ponce Hotel for a gourmet lunch at the renowned **Lola** restaurant (see p87). Don't forget to leave room for ice cream at **King's Cream** (see p87).

Left **La Cruz de Vigía** Right **Casa de la Masacre de Ponce**

Best of the Rest

1 La Cruz de Vigía
This giant hilltop cross soars 98 ft (30 m) and has an observation tower offering fabulous views over Ponce. ◎ *Map F5 • Calle El Vigía Final • Open 9:30am–5pm Tue–Thu, 9:30am–5:30pm Fri–Sun*

2 Museo de la História de Ponce
The museum's exhibits trace the history of Ponce from the 17th century to the present day. ◎ *Map F5 • Calle Isabel 53 • 787 844 7071 • Open 9am–4pm Tue–Sun*

3 Casa de la Masacre de Ponce
Former headquarters of the Nationalist Party, this colonial structure was the site of a massacre by police in 1937 *(see p84)*. ◎ *Map F5 • Calle Marina & Calle Aurora • 787 844 9722 • Open 8am–4:30pm Wed–Sun*

4 Teatro La Perla
This grandiose Neo-Classical theater (1941) features a balcony supported by Corinthian columns. ◎ *Map F5 • Calle Cristina & Calle Mayor • 787 843 4080 • Guided tours: 8am–noon & 1–4:30pm Mon–Fri • Adm*

5 Museo de la Música Puertorriqueña
Browse through traditional Taíno, Spanish, and African musical instruments displayed at this museum, which is housed in a pink building. ◎ *Map F5 • Calle Salud, Ponce • 787 848 7016 • Open 8am–4:30pm Wed–Sun*

6 Guánica
US marines landed at this seaport during the Spanish-American war in 1898. A memorial recalls the event. ◎ *Map D5*

7 Isla Caja de Muertos
This nature preserve protects endemic species and is popular for its beaches and great snorkeling conditions. ◎ *Map G6 • Island Ventures: 787 842 8546*

8 Reserva Nacional Bahía de Jobos
A kayak trail leads you through these mangrove forests, which teem with wildlife. ◎ *Map J6 • Carretera 705 Km 2.3 • 787 853 4617 • Open 9am–4pm*

9 Museo Antigua Aduana
This former Customs House is now a museum dedicated to Samuel Morse, inventor of the Morse code. ◎ *Map K6 • Calle Morse 65, Arroyo • 787 839 8096 • Open 8am–4:30pm Wed–Sun*

10 Baños de Coamo
Many believe in the healing properties of these thermal mineral waters, and often bathe here. ◎ *Map H5 • Carretera 546 Km 1, Coamo • 787 825 1150 • Open 10am–5pm • Adm*

Price Categories

For a three-course meal for one with half a bottle of wine (or equivalent meal), taxes, and extra charges.

$	under $10
$$	$10–$20
$$$	$20–$30
$$$$	$30–$40
$$$$$	over $40

Alexandra's fine interior

Restaurants and Bars

La Cava
Designed to resemble a 19th-century coffee plantation, La Cava has a changing *nouvelle cuisine* menu and a champagne-and-cigar bar. ❧ *Map F5* • *Hilton Ponce, Av Caribe 1150* • *787 259 7676* • *Open 6:30–10:30pm Mon–Sun* • *$$$$*

La Terraza
This alfresco restaurant with lush gardens serves local and international fare and has a great lunch buffet. ❧ *Map F5* • *Hilton Ponce, Av Caribe 1150* • *787 259 7676* • *Open 6:30am–10:30pm Mon–Sun* • *$$$*

Lola
Come and enjoy the eclectic cuisine offered by this classy restaurant. For starters, try the fantastic sampler dish. ❧ *Map F5* • *Ramada Ponce Hotel, Reina St Downtown, Ponce* • *787 813 5033* • *Open 11:30am–11pm Thu–Sat (until 9pm Sun & Mon, 10pm Tue & Wed)* • *$$$*

Alexandra
Creative dishes, such as grilled pork chops with pineapple chutney, are served in an ocean-front setting. ❧ *Map D6* • *Copamarina Beach Resort, Carretera 333 Km 6.5, Caña Gorda* • *787 821 0505* • *Open 6–10:30pm Sun–Thu, 6–11pm Fri–Sat* • *$$$$*

El Ancla
Try the excellent seafood medley at El Ancla, which sits at the end of a pier overhanging the sea. ❧ *Map F5* • *Av Hostos 105, Ponce* • *787 840 2450* • *Open 11am–9:30pm Sun–Thu, 11am–11pm Fri–Sat* • *$$$$*

Rincón Argentino
The cow-sign outside this restaurant gives the game away. This steakhouse in a restored colonial mansion specializes in meats *a la parrillada* (straight from the grill). ❧ *Map F5* • *Calle Salud 64, Ponce* • *787 284 1762* • *Open 11:30am–midnight* • *$$$$*

La Casa del Chef
Visit this place for great local food, with a speciality in grilled meats and seafood. The restaurant also offers an extensive wine list. ❧ *Map F5* • *1307 Callejon Fagot, Ponce* • *787 843 1298* • *Open noon–10pm Tue–Thu (until 9pm Mon, 11pm Fri & Sat)* • *$$*

Seaview Terrace
Enjoy Caribbean dishes served with flair at a candlelit table beneath the stars. ❧ *Map L5* • *Caribe Playa Beach Resort, Carretera 3 Km 112.1, Patillas* • *787 839 6339* • *Open 6–10:30am, noon–3pm & 6:30–9:30pm; dinner by reservation* • *$$$$$*

Costa Marina
This nautically themed restaurant stands on stilts over a mangrove lagoon and serves fresh seafood. ❧ *Map H5* • *Marina de Salinas, Carretera 701 Final, Salinas* • *787 824 5973* • *Open noon–9pm* • *$$$$*

King's Cream
Try free samples of several tropical ice-cream flavors, such as coconut and *guanábana* (soursop), before deciding on one. ❧ *Map F5* • *Calle Marin 9223, Ponce* • *787 843 8520* • *Open 9am–11:50pm* • *$*

Left **A mountain retreat near Utuado** Center **Aibonito** Right **Drive through La Ruta Panorámica**

The Cordillera

ENCOMPASSING THE MOUNTAIN SPINE *that runs the length of Puerto Rico, the Cordillera is accessed by a maze of winding roads that form the Ruta Panorámica. This well-signed route runs past historic plantation homes, lush forest preserves, and pretty lakes, and boasts fabulous views. Although the area's old-fashioned country way of life has given way to modernity, the pace here remains sleepy, enhancing the pleasure of a leisurely drive. The towns of Orocovis and Utuado are famous for their artisans, while Jayuya is a center of ancient Taíno culture. Although accommodations are few, Hacienda Gripiñas, a historic coffee estate, makes a great base for hiking up Cerro Punta, the island's highest peak. To the west lies Maricao, a center of coffee-production renowned for its annual coffee festival.*

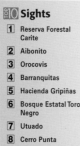

Sights

1. Reserva Forestal Carite
2. Aibonito
3. Orocovis
4. Barranquitas
5. Hacienda Gripiñas
6. Bosque Estatal Toro Negro
7. Utuado
8. Cerro Punta
9. La Ruta Panorámica
10. Maricao

Bosque Estatal Toro Negro

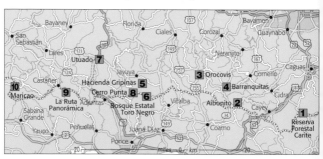

Reserva Forestal Carite

Combining primary and secondary forests, this preserve protects an important watershed in the Sierra de Cayey range. Feathery groves of bamboo and mist-shrouded dwarf forest here are festooned with mosses. This lush world entices with roadside picnic sites and 25 miles (40 km) of trails that are good for hikes and spotting around 50 species of birds, including the endangered endemic mountain hawk. Its proximity to San Juan draws crowds on weekends.
◈ Map K4 • Carretera 184 Km 27.5 • 787 747 4545 • Open 8am–5pm

Reserva Forestal Carite

Aibonito

At 2,400 ft (730 m) above sea level, this is the island's highest town. It is surrounded by alpine pastures – hence its nickname, "Switzerland of Puerto Rico" – and flower-growing is a major industry here. The Neo-Classical Iglesia San José (1897) graces the town's main square and features a gold-leafed wooden altar. The best time to visit is between late June and early July, during the flower festival, when Aibonito is ablaze with anthuriums, begonias, orchids, carnations, and roses. ◈ Map J4

Orocovis

This town is famous for its wood-carvers who produce santos (see p47). Visit the tiny Museo Orocoveño, which honors the craft of saint-carving and also exhibits Taíno artifacts. South of town, the Mirador Orocovis-Villalba is a lookout tower with stunning views of the coast.
◈ Map G4 • Museo Orocoveño: Carretera 155; 787 455 4217; by appointment

Barranquitas

This pretty town is the birthplace of Luis Muñoz Rivera and his son Luis Muñoz Marín (see p31). The elder's home, Casa Muñoz Rivera, is now an interesting museum. The Baroque Iglesia San Antonio de Padua, standing over the town's plaza, has a noteworthy arched ceiling and fine stained-glass windows.
◈ Map H4 • Casa Muñoz Rivera: 787 857 0230; open 8:30am–4:20pm

Barranquitas' main plaza and Iglesia San Antonio de Padua

Coffee

Puerto Rico's gourmet coffee, introduced to the region by Corsican immigrants in the early 1800s, is considered one of the best in the world. The cool, sun-kissed mountains of the southwest boast well-drained, fertile soils – perfect conditions for coffee production. Puerto Rico produces and exports millions of pounds (kilos) of coffee beans.

5 Hacienda Gripiñas

This former coffee estate, built in 1863, enjoys a magnificent setting at a 3,280-ft (1,000-m) elevation, at the base of Cerro Punta. Hikers will love this delightful base for exploring the mountains. The plantation home is now a *parador (see p112)* that offers guided hiking excursions, and coffee grown on the estate is served in the charming restaurant here. Evoking the atmosphere of yester-year, this farm-hotel is worth a visit for a meal, even if you don't choose to stay *(see p117)*.

6 Bosque Estatal Toro Negro

This forest preserve protects over 10 sq miles (28 sq km) of rain-drenched cloudforest, whose waters feed tumultuous rivers and the sierra palms that line the roadside. Trails penetrate the forest from the Doña Juana Recreation Center, where you can pick up area maps. *Coquí* frogs abound, and the endangered Puerto Rican parrot is among the 30 or so bird species to be seen while hiking. Anglers with permits can fish for bass in the numerous lakes. ◈ *Map F4*
• *Doña Juana Recreation Center: Carretera 143 Km 32.4; 787 999 2200; open 7:30am–4:30pm*

7 Utuado

This peaceful town was an important 19th-century center for coffee production, which funded the building of the Neo-Classical Iglesia San Miguel Arcangel, completed in 1878, on the main square. Nearby Lago Caonillas, a serene lake, is a popular week-end escape for city folk seeking peace in the mountains. Reach it via the scenic Carretera 140. En route, stop off at the studio-home of artist couple Miguel and Olga Guzman. ◈ *Map E3 • Studio of Miguel & Olga Guzman: Carretera 140 Km 17.7; 787 894 8765; by appointment*

8 Cerro Punta

At 4,390 ft (1,338 m), this is the tallest peak on the island. It features a *mirador* (lookout tower) from which to enjoy spectacular 360-degree vistas. The steep and narrow access road off Carretera 143 is daunting; park in the gravel lot at the base and hike the 656-ft (200-m) path to the top. The peak is studded with unsightly radio towers, but remains attractive thanks to an abundance of hibiscus bushes. ◈ *Map F4*
• *Carretera 143 Km 16.5*

Hacienda Gripiñas

Share your travel recommendations on **traveldk.com**

Mountain scenery near Utuado

9 La Ruta Panorámica

A scenic route running across the island's mountainous interior, the Ruta Panorámica comprises dozens of roads spanning 166 miles (266 km) between the towns of Yabucoa and Mayagüez. Although convoluted, and with many junctions, the route is well-marked with brown "La Ruta" signs as it dips and rises and twirls through the spectacular landscape. Allow two days to cover the route end to end. You can enjoy simple meals and stock up on snacks at roadside *colmados (see p112)* along the way. ⊗ *Map B4–L5*

10 Maricao

This pleasant town on the western flanks of the cordillera is nestled in the valley of the Río Maricao and surrounded by glossy coffee bushes that carpet the hillsides like green corduroy. Time your visit for mid-February and the annual Festival de la Cosecha del Café (coffee festival), when the town bursts into colorful life with folkloric dancing. Allow time for an intriguing side-trip to the local fish hatchery (Vivero de Peces Maricao), where fish are raised to stock the island's lakes. ⊗ *Map C4 • Maricao Fish Hatchery: Carretera 410 Km 1.7; 787 838 3710; open 8:30–11:30am & 1:30–3:30pm Thu–Sun*

Scenic Drive on La Ruta Panorámica

Day One

🕐 Begin at Yabucoa, in the southeast of the island, and head west along Carretera 182 to 181. From here, follow the "La Ruta" signs as you climb up into the **Sierra de Cayey** and through **Reserva Forestal Carite**, before dropping down to **Cayey** *(see p92)*. Crossing the highway, turn left onto Carretera 1. The route ascends to **Aibonito** – explore the town center before continuing north to **Barranquitas**, with a diversion along Carretera 725 to **Cañon de San Cristóbal** *(see p92)* on the way. Explore the sites at **Barranquitas**, then head west along Carretera 143 to **Bosque Estatal Toro Negro**. Turn north onto Carretera 149 to see the **Salto de Don Juan Cascade**, which can be viewed from the road. A short distance further, turn left onto Carretera 144 for **Hacienda Gripiñas** and stay overnight.

Day Two

Retrace your route to Carretera 143, stopping to visit the **Museo Indígena Cemí** outside **Jayuya** *(see p92)*. Back on Carretera 143, head west to **Cerro Punta**. Hike the access path for good views, then continue along La Ruta to **Adjuntas** *(see p92)* – exit the town on Carretera 518. A web of well-signed, scenic roads leads to **Reserva Forestal Maricao** *(see p92)*, where you can park at trailheads and hike. Descend on Carretera 120 to visit **Maricao** before ending your trip at **Parador Hacienda Juanita**, a charming old coffee estate *(see p92)*.

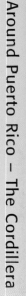

Left **Main plaza at Cayey** Center **Petroglyphs at Piedra Escrita** Right **Museo Indígena Cemí**

Best of the Rest

1 Cayey
This town, a center of tobacco production, is home to a campus of the University of Puerto Rico. The Museo de Arte Dr. Pío López Martínez on the campus displays works by local artists. ◊ Map J4–K4 • Museo de Arte Dr. Pío López Martínez: 787 738 2161, ext 2209; open 8am–4:30pm Mon–Fri, 11am–5pm Sat–Sun

2 Cerro Maravilla
Topped by communications towers, this mountain has two stone crosses marking the site where two *independentistas* were murdered by police on July 25, 1978. ◊ Map F4 • Carretera 577, off Carretera 143

3 Cañon de San Cristóbal
Although difficult to find (ask for directions), this canyon is the deepest gorge in Puerto Rico and features breathtaking cascades. Go on a guided hike. ◊ Map H4 • Carretera 725 Km 5.1, Aibonito • San Cristóbal Hiking Tour: 787 857 2094

4 Jayuya
This town hosts the Festival Indígena each November to celebrate ancient indigenous culture. The Museo Casa Canales regales the region's history. ◊ Map F4 • Museo Casa Canales: Carretera 144 Km 9.2; 787 828 4618; open 9:30am–4:30pm Mon–Fri; Adm

5 Orocovis
This lovely mountain town is known for its popular cultural festivals. ◊ Map G4

6 Museo Indígena Cemí
Visit this museum to see Taíno exhibits, petroglyphs, and artifacts from local archaeological sites. ◊ Map F4 • Carretera 144 Km 9.3 • 787 828 1241 • Open 9am–4pm • Adm

7 Piedra Escrita
This huge rock beside the Río Saliente is engraved with pre-Columbian petroglyphs and can be viewed from a tower. ◊ Map F4 • Piedra Escrita, Carretera 144 Km 2.3

8 Adjuntas
A town in the Valley of the Sleeping Giant, named for a nearby mountain formation, Adjuntas is famous for its citron, which is used in preserves. ◊ Map E4

9 Reserva Forestal Maricao
Admire the beauty of this forest preserve from a hiking trail or from the four-story Torre de Piedra lookout tower on the main highway. ◊ Map C4 • Visitor Center: Carretera 120 Km 16.2 • Open 7am–2:30pm Mon–Fri, 8am–3:30pm Sat–Sun; Torre de Piedra: 8am–4pm

10 Parador Hacienda Juanita
The most beautiful of the old haciendas in Puerto Rico welcomes day visitors. The estate still produces coffee (see p117).

Price Categories
For a three-course meal for one with half a bottle of wine (or equivalent meal), taxes, and extra charges.

$	under $10
$$	$10–$20
$$$	$20–$30
$$$$	$30–$40
$$$$$	over $40

Don Pedro at the historic Hacienda Gripiñas

🔟 Restaurants

1 Casa Bavaria
Visit this festive German beer garden for Teutonic fare, such as bratwurst and sauerkraut. It also serves local dishes and features live music on Saturday. ✆ Map G3 • Carretera 155 Km 38.2, Morovis • 787 862 7818 • Open noon–8pm Sun–Thu, noon–10pm Fri–Sat • $$$

2 Los Avinoes
Enjoy creative Puerto Rican cuisine inside two airplanes, in the midst of Barranquitas' mountains. ✆ Map H4 • Rd #143 Km 57 Helechal Ward, Barranquitas • 787 857 8955 • Open 11am–6pm Mon–Thu (until midnight Fri & Sat, 9pm Sun) • $$

3 Don Pedro
This plantation restaurant at Hacienda Gripiñas (see p117) has a romantic ambience. Stick to the Puerto Rican dishes and end your meal with the estate's coffee. ✆ Map F4 • Open 7–10am & 6–9pm • $$$

4 El Fogón de Abuela
The authentic Puerto Rican fare at this lakeside restaurant includes rabbit dishes, stews, and fricasseed chicken. ✆ Map E3 • Carretera 612 final, Lago Dos Bocas, Utuado • 787 894 0470 • Open noon–7pm Fri, 11:30am–7:30pm Sat–Sun • $$$

5 Casa Grande Café
Enjoy hearty meals and lovely views over lush gardens from the terrace of this colorful restaurant, part of the Casa Grande Mountain Retreat (see p117). ✆ Map E3 • Open 8–10:30am & 5–8pm daily • $$$

6 Aquarium
This modestly elegant restaurant specializes in seafood. It also serves a large selection of other Puerto Rican dishes. ✆ Map E3 • Av Estéves 29, Utuado • 787 894 1500 • Open 11am–8pm Tue–Sun • $$

7 Lechonera el Mojito
Drop in at Guayate's largest lechonera (see p112) for some freshly roasted pork, served with all the trimmings. ✆ Map K4 • Carretera 184 Km 32.9, Guavate • 787 738 8888 • Open 8am–8pm • $$

8 Casona de Juanita
In the Parador Hacienda Juanita (see p117), this restaurant serves simple local dishes, such as cod with fresh vegetables, on a terrace surrounded by trees. ✆ Map C4 • Open 8am–9pm Sun–Thu, 8am–10pm Fri–Sat • $$$$

9 La Fragua
A casual restaurant that has tables with riverside views. Try the special chicken cooked in wine at this casual restaurant. ✆ Map F4 • Bo Coabey Carr. 144 Km 8.8, Jayuya • 787 828 2464 • Open 11am–9pm Fri–Sun • $

10 El Quijote
Home of "The Biggest Burger Challenge", this restaurant offers to give a free meal and a complimentary T-shirt if you finish a 3-lb (1.4-kg) Quijote burger. ✆ Map K4 • Carr. 738 Bo. Montellano, Cayey • 787 738 2598 • Open 4pm–midnight Fri & Sat, noon–7pm Sun • $$

Left **Golf course at Four Points by Sheraton Palmas del Mar Resort** Right **Families at Playa Piñones**

East Coast & Islands

THE EASTERN SIDE OF THE ISLAND *is dramatically different from the rest of Puerto Rico in several regards. It receives the brunt of the rainfall, feeding the lush rain forest of El Yunque, a tropical paradise that offers the island's best hiking. This is the domain, too, of high-end all-inclusive hotels, which are concentrated around Palmas del Mar in the south. The boating center of Fajardo is the gateway for excursions by ferry to the laid-back isles of Vieques and Culebra, which boast Puerto Rico's most sensational beaches and exquisite boutique hotels, and are fast evolving as centers for nature-focused adventure trips.*

Vieques' scenic shoreline

Sights

1. Vieques
2. Culebra
3. El Yunque
4. Playa Piñones
5. Río Grande
6. Luquillo
7. Reserva Natural La Cordillera
8. El Conquistador Resort
9. Reserva Natural Las Cabezas de San Juan
10. Palmas del Mar

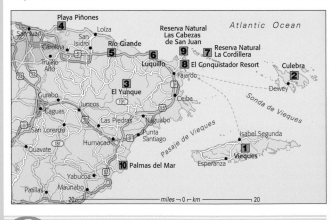

A hiking trail at the lush El Yunque

Vieques

This idyllic island is fringed by fabulous beaches, the best of which became accessible to the public only in the early 2000s, after 50 years of use by the US navy. Parts of the island's wildlife refuge can be accessed by hiking and mountain-biking trails. In the island's only town, Isabel Segunda, locals on horseback outnumber cars, and there is a fort, lighthouse, and an art gallery. Try paddling a kayak at night at Bahía de Bioluminiscente for an experience you'll always remember. Better yet, take a nocturnal dip in the waters and watch yourself glow *(see pp16–17)*.

Culebra

Life on this lovely island, Vieques' smaller twin, revolves around the sleepy village of Dewey. US expatriates operate most businesses in town, many of which offer world-class diving and snorkeling trips. The island's many white-sand beaches include Playa Flamenco *(see p39)*, which is considered to be Puerto Rico's most beautiful. A quarter of Culebra is a wildlife refuge, and is good for spotting marine turtles and birds, and manatees *(see pp18–19)*.

El Yunque

Less than an hour's drive from San Juan, the El Yunque National Forest draws scores of city folk on weekends and holidays to hike well-maintained trails that lead through sodden forests. The lowland rain forest and upland cloudforests teem with birds and riotously noisy coquís. A splendid visitors' center sets the scene for hikes along 36 miles (58 km) of trails, one of which ascends to El Yunque's highest point. Carry along some rain gear when hiking as clouds can form without warning and sudden deluges are common, notably in the afternoon *(see pp14–15)*.

Playa Piñones

Join the picnickers from San Juan at this popular beach on weekends, and dig into local favorites, such as *alcapurria (see p51)*, served at the food shacks here. Traffic jams can be a nightmare, but the 7-mile- (11-km-) long Paseo Piñones Recreational Trail, running along the shore, grants access for pedestrians and cyclists. If you tire of sunning, trails lead into the wetlands inland of the beach. ◈ *Map L2*

A snorkeling trip off the coast of Culebra

5 Río Grande

This beach resort was once a giant coconut and sugarcane plantation. Today it boasts magnificent golf courses and hotels lining lovely beaches. The river after which the resort is named winds through the nearby marshland and mangroves, which can be explored on boat trips. The town of Río Grande comes alive with music and dance during the Carnaval Ciudad de El Yunque, held here each June. ◈ *Map M2*

6 Luquillo

The beauty of this beachside town is enhanced by the brooding Sierra Luquillo mountains, which form a dramatic backdrop. The sand here melds into warm, reef-protected waters that are great for snorkeling. Playa Luquillo has a section known as Mar Sin Barreras, which is equipped for handicapped visitors. Further east, wind-whipped Playa Azul and Playa La Selva are washed by breakers that are good for surfing. ◈ *Map N2 • Mar Sin Barreras: 787 889 4329; open 8:30am–5pm*

7 Reserva Natural La Cordillera

This group of coral cays, sprinkled across the Atlantic in a chain northeast of Fajardo, protects the nesting sites of seabirds and marine turtles. Dolphins are often seen on boat excursions from Fajardo, and the turquoise waters of the preserve are a snorkeler's delight. El Conquistador Resort has an exclusive lease on Isla Palominos, where watersports are offered for guests. ◈ *Map P2 • Erin Go Bragh Sailing and Snorkeling Charters; 787 860 4401; www.egbc.net*

8 El Conquistador Resort

This fabulous hilltop resort in Fajardo overlooks Playa las Croabas and Vieques Sound, and with 910 rooms, is Puerto Rico's largest hotel. Every half an hour, water taxis depart the resort's marina for Isla Palominos, where

El Conquistador Resort's pool area

Reserva Natural Las Cabezas de San Juan

guests can enjoy watersports. The resort boasts a water theme park for guests only, but the hotel's casino and 18-hole golf course are open to the public (see p116).

9 Reserva Natural Las Cabezas de San Juan

This preserve, at the northeast tip of the island, protects lush mangroves and wildlife-rich lagoons. Manatees are seen in Laguna Grande, which glows with bioluminescence at night, and the many bird species found here include osprey, heron, and the Puerto Rican parrot. A trail leads to a lighthouse dating from 1882. ❧ Map N2 • 787 722 5882 • Guided tours only • Adm

10 Palmas del Mar

This gated beachfront resort complex has a marina, shopping areas, tennis courts, an equestrian center, and two championship golf courses, all of which are open to the public. Accommodations at Four Points by Sheraton (see p116) are plush, and there are also rental villas and condominiums. Dive trips are offered from Marina de Palmas. ❧ Map M5 • 787 852 8888 • www.palmasdelmar.com

Day Trip to Vieques

Morning

Start your day early and drive or take a taxi to **Fajardo**, arriving half an hour before the 9:30am ferry departure to **Vieques** (9am on Saturday and Sunday). Alternatively, you can fly to Vieques from San Juan with Vieques Air Link (see p105). In **Isabel Segunda** (see p16) turn left out of the ferry terminal and follow Calle Morropo uphill to the town's light-house and the **Siddhia Hutchinson Art Gallery** (see p17). Return to the waterfront and turn right onto Calle Benítez Guzman and head for Plaza Muñoz Rivera. Here, visit the Spanish-Renaissance style **Parroquia Immaculada Concepción** church, built in 1860, then continue up Calle Fuerte to **Fort Conde Mirasol**, housing the **Vieques Art & History Museum** (see p16), where you can learn about the island's past through interesting exhibits.

Afternoon

Return to the town center and pick up a pre-arranged scooter or Jeep rental. Head south to **Esperanza** (see p16) for a burger or pizza lunch at **Bananas** (see p99). Afterward, drive west, and on Carretera 200, turn left and follow the coast to **Laguna Kiani** (see p17). Take time to explore the mangrove boardwalk before continuing west to **Green Beach** (see p17). Spend the rest of your afternoon snorkeling or simply relax here. Drop in at the island's romantic **Carambola** (see p99) for a candlelit dinner before returning to Isabel Segunda to take the ferry back to Fajardo.

Left **Playa Vacia Talega** Center **A family hiking through El Yunque** Right **The ferry jetty at Vieques**

🔟 Best of the Rest

1 Loíza Aldea
This coastal town began life as a slave settlement and remains a center for Afro-Caribbean culture. The Iglesia Espíritu Santo stands on the town plaza and is the oldest church in continuous use on the island. ❧ *Map M2*

2 Carnival in Loíza Aldea
Loíza Aldea bursts into colorful life in late July for the week-long Festival de Santiago Apóstol, a vibrant celebration of the island's African heritage.

3 Bosque Estatal Piñones
This preserve protects a huge mangrove forest and has hiking trails. Kayaks can be rented to explore the lagoons. ❧ *Map L2*
• *Piñones Ecotours: 787 253 0005*

4 Crab Festival, Maunabo
In late August or early September each year, the town of Maunabo hosts a festival, with live music, street fairs, and stalls selling crab dishes. ❧ *Map L5*

5 Kayaking
Opportunities for kayaking abound at Bahía de Fosforescente on Vieques *(see p110)*, Bosque Estatal Piñones, and Reserva Natural La Cordillera *(see p96)*.

6 Playa Vacia Talega
This beach has ancient sand dunes that were sculpted into fascinating formations by wind and surf and "cemented" in place over eons. ❧ *Map L2*

7 Culebrita
Relax on Playa Tortuga or snorkel in the warm shallows, known as The Baths, at this tiny coral cay *(see p19)*. ❧ *Map R3*
• *Culebrita Adventure Eco-Tour: Ferry Dock, Culebra; 787 930 2111*

8 Sport Fishing
The north coast of Puerto Rico is a prime ground for catching marlin and other gamefish, and the shallows around Vieques and Culebra are good for bonefishing *(see p110)*.

9 Hiking
El Yunque National Forest *(see pp14–15)* has hiking trails that run through various rain forest habitats. For a contrast, hike the subtropical dry forests of Vieques Wildlife Refuge *(see p16)*.

10 Ferry Journey
The 1-hour journey between Fajardo and Vieques or Culebra is magnificently scenic, offering views of El Yunque and the islands of Vieques Sound. Reserve your tickets in advance. ❧ *Ferry terminals: Fajardo: 787 863 3360; Vieques & Culebra: 787 801 0251*

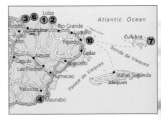

Price Categories

For a three-course meal for one with half a bottle of wine (or equivalent meal), taxes, and extra charges.

$	under $10
$$	$10–$20
$$$	$20–$30
$$$$	$30–$40
$$$$$	over $40

Colorful interior of Bananas

TOP 10 Restaurants

1 Sandy's Seafood Restaurant & Steak House
Despite its simple decor, this steak house draws society figures with its seafood platters, shellfish dishes, and paellas. ◎ Map N2 • Calle Fernandez García 276, Luquillo • 787 889 5765 • Open 11:30am–9pm Wed–Sun • $$$$

2 Blossoms
This stylish oriental restaurant serves sushi and tasty *teppanyaki* dishes. ◎ Map N3 • Av El Conquistador 1000, Fajardo • 787 863 1000 • Open 6–11:30pm • $$$$$

3 Chez Daniel
Visit this restaurant *(see p97)* for its French-inspired dishes, including *escargot*. Leave room for the *soufflé au Cointreau* dessert. ◎ Map M4 • Palmas del Mar, Humacao • 787 850 3838 • Open 6.30–9pm Wed–Sat, noon–4pm & 6:30–9pm Sun • $$$$$

4 Bamboobei
A beachfront restaurant serving seafood and Puerto Rican staples, Bamboobei gets busy on weekends when there's live music. ◎ Map L2 • Carretera 187 Km 4.5, Piñones • 787 253 0948 • Open noon–10pm Wed, Thu & Sun (until 1am Fri & Sat) • $$$

5 Bananas
A part of the Bananas Guesthouse, this lively beach-front restaurant and bar serves tasty burgers, salads, pizzas, steak, and seafood dishes, which can be enjoyed alfresco *(see p113)*. ◎ Open noon–9:30pm • $$$$

6 Chez Shack
This wooden hilltop haunt serves as a bohemian hangout, and buzzes with live reggae music on Wednesday nights. The menu includes barbecued ribs, baked crab, and fish fillets. ◎ Map P5 • Carretera 995 Km 1.8, Esperanza, Vieques • 787 741 2175 • Open 6–11pm Wed–Mon • $$$$

7 Carambola
This fine-dining restaurant exudes romance. Enjoy delicious gourmet Caribbean fusion cuisine by candlelight. ◎ Map P5 • Carretera 996 Km 4.3, Vieques • 787 741 3318 • Open 7–10am & 6–10pm • $$$$$

8 El Quenepo
Experience fine dining at this elegant yet unpretentious restaurant, which overlooks the Esperanza waterfront. ◎ Map P5 • 148 Calle Flamboyan, Vieques • 787 741 1215 • Opens at 5:30pm Tue–Sun • $$$$

9 Brass Cactus
This friendly restaurant is favored for its burgers, Tex-Mex dishes, and stiff drinks. ◎ Map N2 • Carretera 3 Marginal, Luquillo • 787 889 5735 • Open 11am–midnight • $$$

10 Cielito Rosado Cocina Artesanal
Visit this culinary delight at Club Seaborn Boutique for delicious seafood. Try the shrimp in a coconut and curry sauce. ◎ Map Q3 • Club Seabourne Bahía Fulladoza, Culebra • 787 742 3169 • Open 8:30–10:30am & 6–10pm Thu–Sun • $$$

Recommend your favorite restaurant on **traveldk.com**

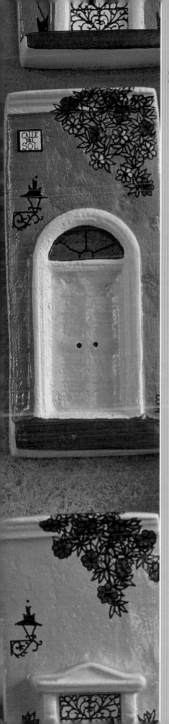

STREETSMART

PUERTO RICO'S TOP 10

Left **Visitors exploring Vieques** Center **A hat for sun protection** Right **Pharmacy**

TOP 10 Planning Your Trip

1 Passports and Visas

All travelers must show a passport. Most European citizens, as well as Japanese and a few others need a non-refundable return ticket from outside the US to qualify for a 90-day visa. Travelers visiting under the Visa Waiver Program must register and pay a fee at https://esta.cbp.dhs.gov. Other nationalities must secure a visa, before traveling, from a US consulate or embassy.

2 Insurance

Get insurance for loss or theft of valuables as well as for medical purposes. Visitors intending to go scuba diving or spelunking must ensure that their policy covers these sports.

3 When To Go

The tourist season runs from December to April. This period is drier and cooler than the rest of the year, although January temperatures still average 77°F (26°C). Adventurous travelers may want to take advantage of low prices during the dangerous yet spectacular hurricane season (see p103).

4 What To Take

Light cottons and breathable, drip-dry synthetics, along with mosquito repellent, sunscreen, and a hat, are recommended. Also carry along smart-casual clothes for dining and nightclubs,

swimwear, and a light jacket for winter nights or for visits to the mountains.

5 How Long To Stay

Most visitors plan a holiday of a week to ten days, including time in San Juan, which takes three days to explore fully. Vieques and Rincón deserve two days each and Ponce, one day. Try to allow two weeks to take in the entire island, including its beaches and highlights from El Yunque to Arecibo.

6 Getting Married

At least two months' advance planning is required to wed in Puerto Rico. You will need to provide passports or identification cards, original notarized copies of birth certificates, and decrees of divorce or a spouse's death, if applicable. Blood tests and a medical examination by a Puerto Rican doctor are also required. Both parties must visit the Register Office to have documents authenticated and to obtain a marriage license, after which the marriage is official.
Ⓢ Demographic Registry Office: 787 728 7980

7 Disabled Travelers

Modern hotels, restaurants, and public buildings have wheelchair access and special bathroom facilities. However, beyond San Juan, few

sidewalks have wheelchair ramps; and obstacles such as potholes are bars to easy mobility. Luquillo Beach (see p96) has a wheelchair ramp.

8 Traveling With Children

Puerto Ricans adore children. Most hotels allow children under 16 to stay with their parents for free; some may charge an extra-bed rate. Items such as baby food and diapers are easily available here. Children's car seats are not offered in rental cars.

9 Inoculations

Puerto Rico poses no serious health risks in terms of infectious diseases, except for dengue fever, which is transmitted by mosquitoes (see p109). No proof of vaccinations is required for travelers, but it is advisable to have up-to-date inoculations for Hepatitis A and B, tetanus, and typhoid.

10 Further Reading

You'll gain a greater appreciation for Puerto Rico by reading about its fascinating history. Several books regale the struggle for independence and the ongoing effort to shape a post-colonial identity. When I was Puerto Rican by Esmeralda Santiago and Puerto Rico in the American Century by César Ayala are recommended.

Preceding pages **Brightly painted souvenir magnets**

Left **Relaxing on the beach in December** Right **A local church**

🔟 General Information

Time Zone
Puerto Rico is 1 hour ahead of US Eastern Standard Time (EST) and 4 hours behind Greenwich Mean Time (GMT). There is no Daylight Saving Time.

Electricity
The electricity supply works mainly on a 110-volt system. Some outlets are 220 volts – these are usually marked. Plugs are the two-pin type, so visitors from Europe may need adaptors. Power cuts are frequent, but most tourist facilities are backed up by generators.

Opening Hours
Shops are usually open 9am–6pm Monday to Saturday; some are also open 11am–5pm on Sunday. Banks open 9am–3:30pm Monday to Friday and 10am–noon on Saturday. Museum hours vary – many are closed on Monday. Most offices and businesses open 8:30am–5:30pm Monday to Friday and close for lunch (noon–1pm).

Public Holidays
Puerto Rico recognizes all US federal holidays in addition to its own commonwealth-established ones. All public offices and many businesses stay closed.

Religion
Puerto Rico is predominantly a Catholic country, although the church plays a limited role in daily life. Every town has a patron saint, and many Puerto Ricans venerate a preferred saint or saints. Adherents of *santería (see p43)* meld Catholic and African religious traditions. About 15 percent of Puerto Ricans are Protestant. Spiritualism is ingrained, especially among the lower-income classes.

Language
Spanish and English are both official languages. Spanish is spoken by everyone, and most people also speak and understand English.

Machismo
Machismo is mostly limited to flirtatious solicitations (often indiscrete or vulgar) to women, but can also include expressions of bravado or even aggression intended to demonstrate male pride.

Climate
Puerto Rico is warm all year round. The best weather occurs from December to April, while the rest of the year is rainier and hotter. Hurricane season is from June to November.

Embassies and Consulates
Many countries maintain consulates in San Juan and can provide assistance to travelers with lost or stolen passports, legal issues, or other emergencies. Canadian and UK consular affairs are handled by offices in Florida. Ⓢ *Canadian Consulate: (305) 579 1600* • *UK Consulate: (305) 371 3500, askmiami@fco.gov.uk*

Gays and Lesbians
Gay and lesbian rights are protected by US federal law. The gay community is fairly overt in cosmopolitan San Juan and Boquerón, while the lesbian scene remains largely hidden. The rest of the island is conservative.

Public Holidays

Jan 1 (New Year's Day); Jan 6 (Epiphany); Jan 11 (Birthday of Eugenio Maria de Hostos); Jan 19 (Martin Luther King Day); Third Mon in Feb (President's Day); Mar 22 (Emancipation Day); Good Friday in Apr; Third Mon in Apr (José de Diego Day); Last Mon in May (Memorial Day); Jul 4 (US Independence Day); Third Mon in Jul (Luis Muñoz Rivera's Birthday); Jul 25 (Constitution Day); Jul 27 (José Celso Barbosa's Birthday); First Mon in Sep (Labor Day); Second Mon in Oct (Columbus Day); Nov 11 (Veterans' Day); Nov 19 (Discovery of Puerto Rico Day); Fourth Thu in Nov (Thanksgiving Day); Dec 25 (Christmas Day)

➡ *Canada and the UK do not have consulates in Puerto Rico.*

Left **A white tourist taxi** Right **A cruise liner at San Juan**

TOP 10 Arriving in Puerto Rico

1 By Air from Europe

Virgin Atlantic offers direct flights once a week between London Gatwick and San Juan. Iberia offers direct flights to Puerto Rico from Madrid. Several major international airlines fly from Europe to Miami and New York, where you can take a connecting flight to Puerto Rico.

2 By Air from North America

Several airlines, such as American Airlines, Delta, and Continental, offer direct flights to Puerto Rico from gateways throughout the US. Air Canada also offers direct services from Canada.

3 Airfares

Airfares vary widely, so compare quotes from Internet suppliers, airlines, and travel agents. Some wholesalers and charter-flight companies offer the best airfare and hotel packages.

4 Luis Muñoz Marín International Airport

San Juan's airport, which is the busiest in the Caribbean, is only a short taxi ride from the city's hotel strip. It has two terminals – the Main Terminal and the American Airlines Terminal – both of which together receive direct flights from more than 20 US cities. Luis Muñoz Marín International

Airport is the Caribbean's main hub for connecting flights to other islands. ◎ Map U2 • 787 791 1014 • www.san-juan-airport.com

5 Other Airports

Some international flights arrive at San Juan's Isla Grande Airport, close to Old San Juan, Condado, and the cruise-ship port. This airport is mainly used for flights to Vieques (see pp16–17) and Culebra (see pp18–19). A few flights also arrive at airports in Aguadilla (see p78), Mayagüez (see p72), and Ponce (see p82). ◎ Isla Grande Airport: Map U2

6 Touts

Hordes of touts often await arriving travelers outside baggage claim, and offer a variety of services such as money exchange, rental cars, and illegal taxis. It is always sensible to decline these offers. Visitors arriving on pre-booked holiday packages are met by bona fide representatives.

7 Changing Money at the Airport

Puerto Rico uses US dollars. If you arrive in possession of Canadian dollars or euros, the airport is a good place to change money. There are foreign exchange bureaus in the arrival halls at San Juan's airport, as well as an ATM, but this may be empty during high season.

8 Airport Taxis

White tourist taxis are available outside baggage claim at each terminal. They charge set rates according to zones – $10 to Isla Verde; $15 to Condado; and $19 to Old San Juan. Several larger hotels offer shuttle-van service for guests. Journey time from the airport to Old San Juan is 30 to 45 minutes, depending on traffic. ◎ Puerto Rico Tourist Taxi • 787 969 3260 • www.cabspr.com

9 Arriving by Sea

San Juan is the home port of more than 20 cruise ships – run by popular cruise lines such as Royal Caribbean and Carnival – that depart for cruises around the Caribbean. A large number of other Caribbean cruise ships include San Juan on their itineraries, and stay one or two nights in port. ◎ Royal Caribbean: www.royalcaribbean.co.uk • Carnival: www.carnival.com

10 Ports of Entry

Official ports of entry for independent sailors are San Juan, Aguadilla, Fajardo, Mayagüez, and Ponce. All arriving vessels must be inspected, and each arriving individual must have a passport and have already completed the online ESTA application or have a valid visa where necessary (see p102).

Left **A rental car** Center **A colorful bus in San Juan** Right **A Cape Air plane**

⑩ Getting Around

1 Internal Flights
Cape Air offers regular connections between Luis Muñoz Marín International and Ponce, Vieques, and Mayagüez. Vieques Air Link flies from Isla Grande Airport to Vieques and Culebra, and Seaborne Airlines links San Juan and Vieques. ◈ *Cape Air: 1800 352 0714 or 508 771 6944; www.capeair.com • Vieques Air Link: 1888 901 9247; www.viequesairlink.com* ◈ *Seaborne Airlines: 877 772 1005 or 787 977 5044; www.seaborneairlines.com*

2 Long-Distance Buses
Although large buses serve metropolitan San Juan, there is no scheduled long-distance service. Travel between island towns is by small *públicos (see below)*. However, private operators like American Tours of Puerto Rico and Rico Sun Tours offer trips around the island in modern, air-conditioned buses with toilets and reclining seats. ◈ *American Tours of Puerto Rico: 787 547 1819 • Rico Sun Tours: 787 722 2080; www.ricosuntours.com*

3 Públicos
Públicos, or gua-guas (buses), are privately operated minibuses that are the staple for travel throughout Puerto Rico. They usually depart from each town's main plaza and can be hailed anywhere along their routes. *Públicos* make frequent stops and are a cheap way to travel locally.

4 City Public Transport
The Metropolitan Bus Authority runs a reliable bus service in San Juan; the brightly colored bus stops are clearly marked "parada" (bus stop) and fares are 75c. The rapid-transit *Tren Urbano*, which connects San Juan's business and Bayamón districts, operates from 5:30am to 11:30pm. There are free trolleys in Old San Juan and Isla Verde districts, and in downtown Ponce. Elsewhere, *públicos* provide bus services. ◈ *Metropolitan Bus Authority • 787 767 7979 • www.dtop.gov.pr/ama/rutas.htm*

5 Taxis
Taxis are easily available within San Juan and major cities. Fares within San Juan are zoned. Not all non-zoned taxi drivers use their meters, preferring to charge a set fare. *Linéas* (or *colectivos*) – private taxis in which you share rides with other passengers – operate in many towns.

6 Car Rental
Most major car rental companies have offices at the airport, in San Juan, and in larger cities. It is wise to reserve a car ahead of your arrival. Scooters can be rented on Vieques and Culebra.

7 Driving
Driving in Puerto Rico requires extreme caution. While the island has an extensive road system and good signage, many drivers disregard traffic regulations and towns can get congested. When trying to find a destination, be aware that the Km figure in an address is a distance marker.

8 Walking
Walking is the best way of exploring Old San Juan and Ponce's historic downtown, so remember to wear comfortable shoes. It is advisable to carry drinking water.

9 By Bicycle
The serene islands of Vieques and Culebra, and the Rincón area, are ideal for exploring by bicycle. You can rent one from Vieques Adventure Company. *(See also p36.)* ◈ *Vieques Adventure Company • 787 692 9162*

10 By Boat
The Port Authority's ferries depart Fajardo for the islands of Vieques and Culebra several times daily, but there is no service between Vieques and Culebra. Car ferries also serve the two islands. Private boats can be chartered at marinas. ◈ *Puerto Rican Port Authority • Fajardo: 800 981 2005 or 800 863 0852; Vieques: 787 741 4761; Culebra: 787 741 3161*

> Rental cars are not permitted on the Puerto Rican Port Authority car ferries that serve Vieques and Culebra.

Left **Store selling local publications** Right **International and local newspapers and magazines**

TOP10 Sources of Information

1 Tourist Offices Abroad

The Puerto Rico Tourism Company has offices in the US, Canada, UK, and Spain that provide brochures, maps, and general information on attractions, activities, and accommodations. For more detailed information, consult independent travel agencies and websites (see below). ✆ *Puerto Rico Tourism Company: 800 866 7827 (US)* • *(416) 368 2680 (Canada)* • *www.seepuertorico.com*

2 Local Tourist Offices

There are local tourist offices scattered around the country, with the main Puerto Rico Tourism Company information bureau in San Juan. Specialist tour operators are also good sources for maps, brochures, and personalized travel advice. There are very few tourist information offices outside San Juan. ✆ *Puerto Rico Tourism Company: Map V6; La Casita, Pier 1, Old San Juan; 721 2400 (San Juan)* • *841 8044 (Ponce)* • *823 5024 (Rincón)* • *787 741 0800 (Vieques)* • *www. gotopuertorico.com*

3 Local Tour Operators

Found throughout the country, local tour operators are often the most reliable sources of information about

sightseeing and activities related to specific regions and destinations. Hotel tour desks will be able to provide details of local organized tours and activities.

4 Websites

A huge amount of information about the country is available online. Google and other search engines are useful means of locating any specific information you may need, such as weather conditions, the cost of flights, or the availability of sporting activities. Try logging on to www.seepuertorico. com, www.puertoricoday trips.com, and http:// welcome.topuertorico.org.

5 Maps

There are several good maps of the country, the best published by International Travel Maps and Books. The best outlet for maps in San Juan is Cronopios. ✆ *International Travel Maps and Books: www.itmb.com* • *Cronopios: Map U6; Calle San Jose 255, San Juan; 787 724 1815*

6 English-Language Newspapers

The *Puerto Rico Daily Sun* is the only English-language daily newspaper published on the island. The weekly *Qué Pasa Magazine* has useful tourist information, and *The Vieques Times* is published monthly.

7 Local Publications

Several daily Spanish-language newspapers compete, including *El Nuevo Día*, *Vocero*, and *Primera Hora*. Several towns also publish their own local newspapers – most are available online.

8 Bookstores

Several bookstores in San Juan, such as La Tertulia, have a good range of guidebooks, maps, and other travel-related literature. Hotel gift stores are also good sources. ✆ *La Tertulia: Map V6; 305 Recinto Sur, Old San Juan; 787 724 8200*

9 Guides

There are many well-informed and qualified guides available in Puerto Rico, although some individuals offering their services can be a nuisance. Ask your hotel concierge or local travel agencies for a recom-mended and reliable guide. Many taxi drivers also hire themselves out as guides.

10 Libraries

San Juan's Biblioteca Nacional has a vast array of books, maps, and documents, but they are mainly in Spanish. Most of the other towns also have libraries. ✆ *Biblioteca Nacional: Map W6* • *Av Ponce de León 500, San Juan* • *787 725 1060* • *Open 8am–4:30pm*

Left **Local phone card** Center **A public phone booth** Right **Credit card**

🔟 Banking and Communications

The US Dollar

The US dollar ($) is the local currency, sometimes referred to as the peso or dolar by locals. The dollar is divided into 100 cents (centavos or chavitos to locals), with coins in denominations of 1, 5, 10, 25, and 50 cents, and notes of 1, 2, 5, 10, 20, 50, and 100 dollars in circulation.

Foreign Currencies

Some tourist entities may accept payment in Canadian dollars and Euros, although these are the exception. Major foreign currencies can be exchanged on the island at banks, casas de cambios (see below), and hotel reception desks.

Banks and ATMs

Puerto Rico has many US- and foreign-owned, as well as local, banks. Most will change foreign currencies at the official rate. Opening hours are typically 9am–3:30pm Monday to Friday. Major banks, such as Banco Popular, Banco de San Juan, and Citibank, operate ATMs that accept MasterCard and Visa.

Casas de Cambio

These currency exchange bureaus are relatively few. They offer more or less the same rate as banks, usually cash traveler's checks, and have longer hours than banks. The Thomas

Cook Foreign Exchange at Luis Muñoz Marín International Airport and the Caribbean Foreign Exchange in Old San Juan are reliable. ⬥ Thomas Cook Foreign Exchange: Map U2; Luis Muñoz Marín International Airport; 787 791 1960 • Caribbean Foreign Exchange: Map U6; Calle Tetuán 201B, Old San Juan; 787 722 8222

Credit Cards

Major credit cards are widely accepted in hotels, restaurants, and tourist-oriented stores, but not in colmados (see p112) and other out-of-the-way stores. Credit cards can be used for cash advances at banks, though you may be charged a commission. You can also use them at ATMs, so carry your personal identification number (PIN) before leaving for your trip.

Telephones

Puerto Rico has an efficient telephone system. Public phones are ubiquitous and prepaid phone cards are easily available. Calls from hotels can be expensive. To call the island from North America, dial 1, then 787 and the local number; from the UK, dial 00 for international access, followed by 01, then 787 and the local number. All phone numbers within Puerto Rico have a 3-digit area code, either 787 or 939. So dial all 10 digits for calls within the island.

Cell Phones

AT&T Mobility and Claro (the wireless arm of the Puerto Rico Telephone Company) offer cellular services throughout the island. However, don't count on your cell phone working in some of the relatively remote locations.

Post Offices

The US Postal Service extends to Puerto Rico, where US rates apply and service is speedy and efficient. Every town has a post office. Check with the reception staff of your hotel to see if they can forward your mail to the post office.

Internet

Many of the larger hotels provide a complimentary Internet service, while others charge a fee. An increasing number of hotels have a Wi-Fi service. Internet cafés are widely available and charge reasonable rates.

Television and Radio

Most hotels include cable TV in room rates, with international channels such as CNN and the BBC, along with local Spanish-language ones. Premium channels may be available on a pay-per-view basis. Qué Pasa TV, available in metro area hotels, broadcasts tourist information. Most radio stations are Spanish language.

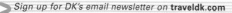

Left **Umbrella sun protection** Center **Beware of pickpockets** Right **Local police**

ᵀᴼᴾ10 Security and Health

1 Emergencies
In an emergency, dial 911 for fire, police, or medical assistance. Hotels can also arrange for a doctor in an emergency. Major disasters, such as hurricanes and floods, are handled by Puerto Rico Emergency Management Agency.

2 Health Services
Local health standards are comparable with those of the US mainland. There are doctors and hospitals in all cities, and clinics in smaller towns. Many large hotels have nurses on staff. Your hotel may also be able to recommend an English-speaking doctor. Invest in insurance for travel, as fees for medical services can be high. Most US health-insurance plans are accepted.

3 Pickpockets
Plenty of tourists get lulled into a false sense of security and are victims of pickpocketing or opportunistic snatch-and-grab theft. Avoid wearing jewelry in public, keep wallets in a secure pouch, and keep your valuables in a hotel safe.

4 Personal Safety
The US State Department issues no special travel advisories for Puerto Rico, where violent crime against tourists is extremely rare. However, muggings have occurred at night on San Juan's Condado and Isla Verde beaches. Stay alert when walking along the back streets of San Juan and the area around Old San Juan's cemetery and La Perla district. There is scant regard for traffic regulations, so be sure to drive carefully.

5 Harassment
Many visitors may experience some level of harassment in tourist areas, from touts offering services or selling trinkets. Rudeness rarely produces a satisfactory outcome – a firm "no" should suffice. Should you wish to lodge a formal complaint, call 1800 866 7827.

6 Police
Tourist police patrol Old San Juan, as well as Condado and Isla Verde. Every town has a local police station. Be aware that low-ranking offices may not have English-speaking staff.

7 Sunstroke
The tropical sun is intense, so make sure you use sunscreen with a high UV factor, plus a hat, sunglasses, and long-sleeved shirts. Avoid the midday sun. See a doctor if, after sun exposure, you feel nauseous, dizzy, or chilled.

8 Women Travelers
Women can receive a fair amount of unwanted attention from Puerto Rican men. Usually it takes the form of harmless, though sometimes vulgar, comments. Avoid remote beaches and walking alone at night.

9 Prescription Medicines
It is always a good idea to bring along enough prescription medications to last the duration of your stay. Still, pharmacies are ubiquitous in Puerto Rico and there should be no problem getting refills should the need arise.

10 Water and Food Hygiene
Tap water is said to be safe to drink, but try to stick to bottled water. Food hygiene is generally good, but avoid food that has been in the sun or stood too long on a buffet counter.

Directory

Emergencies
• Police: 787 343 2020
• Puerto Rico Emergency Management Agency: 787 729 7637

Hospitals
• Ashford Presbyterian Community Hospital, San Juan; Map X1–X2; 787 721 2160
• Perea Hospital, Mayagüez; Map B4; 787 834 0101
• Dr. Pila Hospital, Ponce; Map F5; 787 848 5600

Left **A crowded beach** Center **Bottles of rum** Right **A warning sign at the beach**

🔟 Things to Avoid

1 Traffic Jams
Rush-hour traffic is notoriously bad in San Juan, which can get appallingly congested, as can almost every other town in Puerto Rico. Traffic jams are common at popular beach resorts, especially on weekends and public holidays. At these times, congestion is particularly bad when re-entering San Juan from the east.

2 Taxi Scams
Tourist taxis in San Juan operate within zones with pre-fixed rates (see p105). Elsewhere on the island, including metropolitan San Juan, the taxis use meters. For longer journeys and sightseeing, you will have to negotiate a fare with the driver before you set off. Most are honest, but there are a few who will attempt to bamboozle you out of large sums. Ask your hotel concierge for an appropriate fare.

3 Running Out of Cash
Banks in Puerto Rico are usually closed on weekends, and ATMs often run out of cash The *casas de cambio* (see p107) are more flexible, but are relatively few in number. So make sure you are carrying enough cash, especially on weekends or if you are going to the countryside or mountains.

4 Money-Changing Scams
Avoid people offering to exchange foreign currency for US dollars. There have been many incidences of tourists being robbed or short-changed by touts and unscrupulous money-changers.

5 Mosquitoes
Although mosquitoes in Puerto Rico do not carry malaria, they can transmit dengue fever – a viral infection for which there is no vaccine. To avoid being bitten, use insect repellent containing DEET and wear light-colored clothing. Long-sleeved shirts and full-length pants also help, as can a ceiling fan above your bed.

6 Sand Fleas
Irritating and miniscule sand fleas, commonly called "no-see-ums", are a nuisance on beaches around dusk and sometimes at dawn. Their bites itch terribly. Insect repellents rarely work, but Avon Skin-so-Soft is effective, so take some along.

7 Crowded Beaches
If it is a relaxing time you are after, then the popular beaches are best avoided on weekends and public holidays, when they become packed with families and tourists. This is especially true of beaches east of San Juan, which are disgustingly littered after the crowds depart. Try to go mid-week.

8 Rip Tides
These dangerous, fast-moving undertows are common on beaches that receive high surf. They are difficult to detect and can change location. Always check with locals about tidal conditions before swimming. If caught in an undertow, swim parallel to the beach to escape.

9 Alcohol
Avoid consuming alcohol during the day as it can cause dehydration. If you do indulge, be sure to also drink plenty of water. Never drink if you intend to drive; drink driving is a major problem in Puerto Rico and penalties are severe if you are caught.

10 Drugs
Although Puerto Rico has less of a drugs culture than many Caribbean islands, drug dealers are present in some tourist resorts and nightclubs, and drug trafficking has contributed to an escalating crime wave. Corrupt Puerto Rican police have been implicated in trafficking, yet most police take a very harsh view of drug use. Buying and dealing drugs is both avoidable and dangerous – getting caught will do more than ruin your vacation.

Left **Trolleys make sightseeing easier on hot days in San Juan** Right **Kayaking**

Tours and Special Interests

1 Tours of San Juan

Although the best way to explore San Juan is on foot, free trolleys make sightseeing easier on hot days, although there is no narration. Also popular are Segway tours of the city, which run to 45 minutes or 2 hours and are narrated in English. Rent a Bicycle *(see p36)* runs fun bike tours. By night, a guided walking tour with Legends of Puerto Rico brings the past back to life. ⬡ *Segway Tours: www.segwaytourspr.com • Legends of Puerto Rico: www.legendsofpr.com*

2 Excursions to Vieques & Culebra

Day trips are a great way of sampling Vieques *(see pp16–17)* and Culebra *(see pp18–19)*. East Island Excursions offers daily trips to Culebra aboard a high-speed cata-maran, and nightly trips to Vieques to see the Bahía de Bioluminiscente. ⬡ *East Island Excursions: www.eastwindcats.com*

3 Day Trips and Activities

Puerto Rico is small enough to explore on day trips from San Juan, and many companies offer excursions. Erin Go Bragh offers snorkeling and sailing trips to the Palominos Islands, which lie to the northwest of Fajardo. Other trips include kayaking in Laguna Grande, and

hiking in El Yunque *(see pp14–15)*. ⬡ *Erin Go Bragh: www.egbc.net • Kayaking Puerto Rico: www.kayakingpuertorico.com*

4 Spanish-Language Schools

Visitors keen to learn Spanish have plenty of opportunity to do so in Puerto Rico. Several language schools offer programs in San Juan and elsewhere on the island. ⬡ *Spanish Abroad: www.spanishabroad.com/sanjuan.htm*

5 Bird-Watching

Puerto Rico is an ideal bird-watching destination. Despite its small size, it is home to some 350 bird species, including 17 endemic species, and 25 species that are endemic to other Caribbean isles *(see p37)*. ⬡ *Amazilia Tours • www.amaziliatours.com*

6 Sport Fishing

The waters off Puerto Rico are world-renowned for superb marlin fishing. The Mona Passage is good for dorado, marlin, and tuna. Several charter boats offer sport-fishing trips *(see p36)*. ⬡ *Parguera Fishing Charters: www.puertoricofishing charters.com • Wild Fly Charters, Vieques: www.wildflycharters.com*

7 Surfing

Puerto Rico offers tremendous surfing year-round, although the best

surfing season is October through mid-April. Rincón is regarded one of the best surf spots in the world, with waves exceeding 30 ft (10 m) *(see p36)*. ⬡ *Rincón Surf & Board • www.surfandboard.com*

8 Scuba Diving

Scuba diving off Puerto Rico is an exhilarating experience. Coral reefs stretch along almost 300 miles (500 km) of coastline. The north coast offers spectacular wall dives. Go through a diving company – you'll find several around the island *(see p36)*. ⬡ *www.pureadventure puertorico.com • Culebra: www.culebradivers.com • Vieques: www.black beardsports.com • Isla Desecheo: www.tainodivers.com*

9 Whale-Watching

Humpback whales pass through the Mona Passage in winter. Whale-watching trips set out from Rincón, which has a tailor-made lookout area *(see p55)*. ⬡ *Taino Divers: www.tainodivers.com*

10 Gourmet Dining

The local culinary scene fuses traditional island ingredients with international cooking techniques, resulting in world-class dining. There are plenty of gourmet restaurants throughout the isle, and especially in San Juan *(see pp48–9)*.

Left **A street stall** Center *Públicos* Right **Local souvenirs**

🔟 Budget Tips

1 Low-Season Travel
You can save a good deal of money by visiting between June and mid-December. This is the hurricane season, so prices are lower for hotels and car rental, and sometimes for airfares.

2 Street Food
Food prepared at street stalls and beach grills, or in *colmados (see p112)*, is usually an excellent bargain. Often a plate of barbecued chicken or pork served with rice, black beans, and *plátanos* will cost less than $5. Some of the best street fare is at Playa Piñones *(see p49)*. Make sure your meal has been freshly cooked and hasn't been sitting out in the sun for too long.

3 Haggling
Most street stalls and souvenir stores mark up prices beyond what may be reasonable for crafts, necklaces, and other souvenirs. Haggling over a fair price is an accepted way of doing business, and essential to getting a good bargain. Expect to negotiate a reduction of 10–20 percent of the asking price.

4 Avoid Tourist Stores
Shops and souvenir stores in hotels and tourist-oriented malls are often overpriced. Unless the quality is exceptional, you're much better off buying souvenirs at crafts markets. General items, such as toiletries, will be cheaper at neighborhood *colmados (see p112)*.

5 Public Transport
Públicos and *guaguas (see p105)* are a fraction of the price of hiring a car or using taxis, and offer visitors the advantage of getting to mingle with locals. Although not as comfortable as taking your own transport, they are usually reliable and will get you to your destination very inexpensively.

6 Package Tours
Package tours can offer tremendous value and are usually far less expensive than booking airfares, hotels, and perhaps car rental separately yourself. Unlike on escorted group tours, you travel independently on a package tour and can often choose from several all-inclusive options at different prices to suit your budget.

7 Phone Cards
Most hotels charge exorbitant rates for calls made from guest rooms. You can save a considerable amount of money by buying a prepaid phone card in various denominations for use in public phones and sometimes even in hotel rooms. These are available in shops, supermarkets, and drugstores.

8 All-Inclusives
If you plan to spend most of your time at the beach and are not interested in dining around or exploring far and wide, consider checking into an all-inclusive resort hotel. These properties charge a single rate that includes your accommodation, meals, entertainment, and use of the hotel's facilities. Exactly what is included can vary from hotel to hotel, so check the fine print before making your choice.

9 Happy Hours
Many bars and restaurants offer an early-evening happy hour, usually between 6pm and 8pm, when cocktails and other drinks are sold at half price, sometimes accompanied by complimentary snacks. Also look for other specials, such as "Ladies Night," when women receive half-price drinks, two-for-ones, and even free admission to nightclubs.

10 Special Discounts
Surf the Internet for travel discounts. Many airlines and tour companies offer last-minute price reductions, but this may mean you have to leave at short notice. Some museums offer free or discounted entry on certain days. And look for promotional specials, frequently offered by newly opened shops, bars, and restaurants.

Left **Fresh fruit and vegetables** Right *Lechoneras*

🔟 Eating and Accommodation Tips

1 Colmados and Fondas
These brightly painted general stores scattered throughout the country sell pastries, sandwiches, and cheap meals – usually simple local dishes such as *fricase* (stew) or roast chicken with rice and beans. An interesting alternative is to savor a hearty, inexpensive lunch at a *fonda*, a simple workmen's café.

2 Fresh Fruit and Vegetables
There is no shortage of delicious tropical fruit to be enjoyed in Puerto Rico, but be sure to peel or thoroughly wash the food items before eating. Salads and other raw preparations in higher-end establishments are usually safe to eat, but should be avoided in *colmados* and *fondas*.

3 Bills and Tipping
Most upscale restaurants include a 10–15 percent service charge in the bill. This may or may not find its way to the staff serving you, so feel free to leave an additional 10 percent if the service warrants it.

4 Lechoneras
Puerto Ricans are fanatical about pork, their favorite dish, which is best enjoyed at a *lechonera* (an open-air roadside restaurant, where whole suckling pigs are spit-roasted).

Most of these restaurants are open Friday through Sunday and are popular among locals during public holidays.

5 Alcoholic Drinks
Most international brands are available in Puerto Rico, but local beers and liquors are as good as any. Try the refreshing lager-style Criolla, Medalla, Silver Key Light, and India beers. Rums are aged for three ('white" or *carta Blanca*), five ("golden" or *dorado*), and seven or more ("aged" or *añejo*) years – the older the better. A tour of the Bacardi rum distillery *(see p62)* provides a primer.

6 All-Inclusives
These large resort hotels are ideal for vacationers who prefer all the hotel costs to be included in a single rate *(see p111)*. Most of them offer buffet meals and a choice of one or more à la carte restaurants. They usually offer watersports and entertainment too, and can be a great way to enjoy a beach vacation at bargain rates.

7 Hotel Tax
All regular tourist hotels levy a 9 percent hotel tax, which you will find added to your bill. *Paradores (see below)* charge 7 percent, while resort hotels add an 11 percent tax on room rates.

8 Accommodation Types
Accommodations in San Juan range from charming colonial hotels with period furnishings to international-style modern beach resorts and casino hotels. There are also a few cheap guesthouses and apartments. Large all-inclusives line much of the north coast. Up in the mountains, there are country inns and guesthouses offering cozy, albeit simple, lodgings. Vieques is known for its trendy boutique hotels.

9 Paradores
Paradores are family-owned and operated inns outside San Juan. They range from centuries-old haciendas to small properties in out-of-the-way coastal villages. Although promoted for their intimacy, many are barely distinguishable from soulless motels, so if you plan on staying in one, try to check up on it before making reservations.

10 Reservations
It is advisable to book at least your first few nights prior to your arrival. During high season *(see p102)*, it is wise to reserve all your accommodations well in advance, as the island gets very crowded. You can usually travel around during low season without pre-booking.

Price Categories

For a standard,
double room per
night (with breakfast
if included), taxes,
and extra charges.

$	under $50
$$	$50–100
$$$	$100–150
$$$$	$150–250
$$$$$	over $250

Hotel Meliá's reception

🔟 Budget Hotels

1 Hotel Milano
The non-smoking rooms are comfortable in this renovated 19th-century warehouse in the heart of Old San Juan, close to the cruise dock. The open-air rooftop restaurant offers waterfront views. ◎ *Map V6 • Calle Fortaleza 307, Old San Juan • 787 729 9050 • www.hotel milanopr.com • $*

2 Doubletree by Hilton San Juan
Handily close to the beach, this chain hotel comes with modern amenities and facilities. What it lacks in style it makes up for in cleanliness and bargain rates.
◎ *Map X2 • Calle de Diego 105, Condado • 787 721 1200 • www.doubletree1. hilton.com • $$$*

3 El Canario Inn
This informal Spanish-style bed-and-breakfast is one block from Condado beach and is handy for nearby restaurants. Air-conditioned rooms have cable TVs, telephones, and ceiling fans.
◎ *Map W2 • Av Ashford 1317, Condado, San Juan • 787 722 3861 • www. canariohotels.com • $$$*

4 Hotel y Parador Mayagüez Bay
A modern, no-frills downtown high-rise, formerly in the *parador* system, El Sol caters mainly to business travelers but is perfectly positioned for exploring

the southwest. It has a swimming pool, friendly staff, and modest, spacious non-smoking rooms. ◎ *Map B4 • Calle Santiago Riera Palmer 9, Mayagüez • 787 834 0303 • $$*

5 Lazy Parrot
This delightful and unpretentious mountain retreat has a swimming pool located on a hillside, colorful decor, and cozy rooms with balconies. You can dine on tasty fare at the open-air restaurant here. ◎ *Map A3 • Carretera 413 Km 4.1, Rincón • 787 823 5654 • www.lazyparrot.com • $$*

6 Fajardo Inn
Popular as a budget alternative to the El Conquistador *(see p116)*, this motel-style lodge sits atop a hill over-looking Fajardo. Its clean, spacious bedrooms have modest furnishings, and most have fine views.
◎ *Map N3 • Parcela Beltrán 52, Fajardo • 787 860 6000 • www.fajardoinn.com • $$*

7 Coquí Inn
Appealing to travelers who don't seek luxuries, this budget hotel adorned with murals is close to Isla Verde beach. Its air-conditioned rooms have cable TV and free WiFi. Some of the rooms are equipped with kitchens.
◎ *Map U2 • Calle Mar Mediterraneo, Isla Verde San Juan • 787 726 4330 • www.coqui-inn.com • $*

8 Hotel Meliá
This family-run centenary Art Deco hotel, located in Parque Degetau in the historic heart of Ponce, is known for its gourmet restaurant *(see p87)*. Rooms are clean and cozy, albeit inelegantly furnished. Period details add charm to the public areas. The hotel has a swimming pool. ◎ *Map F5 • Calle Cristina & Plaza Degetau, Ponce • 787 842 0260 • www.hotelmeliapr.com • $$*

9 Parador Guánica 1929
This historic hotel over looking the Caribbean sea has modestly furnished rooms with satellite TVs and kitchenettes. The facilities include a swimming pool, basketball court, and children's pool. ◎ *Map D5 • Carretera 3116 Km 2.5, Guánica • 787 821 0099 • www.tropicalinnspr.com/ guanica-1929.php • $$*

10 Bananas Guesthouse
This charming, beach-front hotel has a popular open-air bar-restaurant *(see p99)*. Its small but cozy rooms have ceiling fans, but lack TVs and phones. It makes for a perfect escape for the island's laid-back crowd. ◎ *Map P5 • Calle Flamboyan Esperanza, Vieques • 787 741 8700 • www.bananasguesthouse. com • $$*

Left **Plush room at the Gallery Inn** Right **El San Juan Hotel & Casino**

TOP 10 San Juan Hotels

1 Hotel El Convento
Exuding 18th-century charm, this former 17th-century convent has deluxe rooms, a superb restaurant, and a splendid location in the heart of Old San Juan. The romantic, individually styled rooms have elegant period furnishings. ◈ Map U6 • Calle del Cristo 100, Old San Juan • 787 723 9020 • www.elconvento.com • $$$$$

2 The Gallery Inn
Comprising three restored 18th-century town houses, this hotel offers elegance and luxury. Its rooms are adorned with antiques and whimsical trompe l'oeil walls. Enjoy splendid views over Old San Juan from the rooftop deck. ◈ Map V5 • Calle Norzagaray 204, Old San Juan • 787 722 1808 • www.thegalleryinn.com • $$$$$

3 Hotel Miramar
This charming hotel is located in one of San Juan's oldest residential neighborhoods, not far from the Puerto Rico Convention Center, eateries, and shops. The in-house restaurant features local and international cuisine, and the beach is only a short walk away. Children under 12 stay for free. ◈ Map T1/T2 • Av Ponce de León 606, Miramar • 787 977 1000 • www.miramar hotelpr.com • $$

4 Sheraton Old San Juan Hotel & Casino
This high-rise has a faux-colonial exterior and very modern interiors. The stylish, non-smoking rooms are comfortable. It offers a choice of restaurants, plus a casino and rooftop pool. ◈ Map V6 • Calle Brumbaugh 100, Old San Juan • 787 721 5100 • www.sheratonold sanjuan.com • $$$$

5 San Juan Marriott Resort & Casino
The Marriott is a high-rise, full-service resort hotel. The pool has a waterslide, and the casino and restaurants draw wealthy locals. The rooms are well furnished and have flat-screen HDTV; some also have ocean views. ◈ Map W2 • Av Ashford 1309, Condado • 787 722 7000 • www.marriott.com • $$$$

6 Caribe Hilton
This historic hotel has a private beach and offers a choice of rooms, from studios to deluxe villas with kitchens, all state-of-the-art amenities. It also has a spa. ◈ Map T1 • Calle Los Rosales, Condado • 787 721 0303 • www.hiltoncaribbean.com • $$$$

7 El San Juan Hotel & Casino
San Juan's signature hotel is loaded with facilities, including nine restaurants, three swimming pools, and a casino. The rooms are styled in tropical colors. The opulent Palm Lobby is a great place for cocktails. ◈ Map U2 • Av Isla Verde 6063, Isla Verde • 787 791 1000 • www3.hilton.com • $$$$

8 Ritz Carlton, San Juan Hotel, Spa, & Casino
The city's premier resort offers rooms with classical European styling. Its ritzy facilities include a casino, tennis courts, and spa. ◈ Map U2 • Av Los Gobernadores 6961, Isla Verde • 787 253 1700 • www.ritzcarlton.com • $$$$$

9 Radisson Ambassador Plaza Hotel
This hotel, a short stroll from the beach, is all non-smoking. The rooms are eclectic, with influences ranging from Art Deco to imperial China. It also has a casino. ◈ Map W2 • Av Ashford 1369, Condado • 787 721 7300 • www.radisson.com • $$$

10 Condado Plaza Hotel & Casino
Fitness buffs will appreciate this hotel's private beach, tennis courts, pool, and well-equipped gym. The suave rooms have minimalist furnishings. There is a 24-hour casino. ◈ Map T1 • Av Ashford 999, Condado • 787 721 1000 • www.condadoplaza.com • $$$

Price Categories

For a standard, double room per night (with breakfast if included), taxes and extra charges.

$	under $50
$$	$50–100
$$$	$100–150
$$$$	$150–250
$$$$$	over $250

Restaurant at the Water & Beach Club

TOP 10 Boutique Hotels

1 Numero Uno Guesthouse

This renovated 1940s home has rooms with cable TV, high-speed Internet, and cream and taupe decor. Some rooms have ocean views. Cocktails are served here, and the gourmet restaurant is renowned. ◈ Map T1 • Calle Santa Ana 1, San Juan • 787 726 5010 • www.numero1guest house.com • $$$

2 The Water & Beach Club

A trendy hotel with a chic minimalist theme, where blue neon is ubiquitous and a waterfall against a gunmetal wall adds to the aqueous theme. Two gourmet restaurants and a hip bar draw urban sophisticates at night. ◈ Map U2 • Calle Tartak 2, Isla Verde • 787 265 6699 • www.waterbeachclub hotel.com • $$$$

3 El Prado Inn

The Andalusian-Moorish decor at this restored 1930s mansion extends to the garden patio, which has a plunge pool. Rooms have cool colonial-style tiles and Mediterranean furnishings. ◈ Map S1 • Calle Luchetti 1350, San Juan • 787 391 1976 • www.elpradoinn.net • $$$

4 Chateau Cervantes

A 16th-century facade hides this hotel's suave contemporary decor. All 12 suites have flat-panel TVs, free WiFi. The hotel's restaurant serves gourmet fare and has an extensive wine list. ◈ Map V6 • Recinto Sur 329, Old San Juan • 787 724 7722 • www. cervantespr.com • $$$$$

5 Hotel Horned Dorset Primavera

Named for a breed of English sheep, this aristocratic hacienda-style hotel, which has its own beach, has suites decorated with plantation style antiques. The gourmet restaurant draws diners from as far as San Juan – a dress code applies in the evening (see p49). ◈ Map B3 • Carretera 429 Km 3, Rincón • 787 823 4030 • www.horneddorset. com • $$$$$

6 Hacienda Tamarindo

The owner, an interior designer, shows her skills in the 17 individually styled suites at this lovely hilltop hotel, which has a tamarind tree in the atrium lobby. There is a tropical theme throughout. ◈ Map P5 • Carretera 996 Km 4.5, Vieques • 787 741 0420 • www.hacienda tamarindo.com • $$$$

7 Club Seabourne

This reclusive hillside property is surrounded by lush lawns dotted with fruit trees. Its rooms cottages, and large villas sport colonial-style furnishings. There is a swimming pool, plus free use of kayaks. ◈ Map Q3 • Fulladoza Bay, Culebra • 787 742 3169 • www. clubseabourne.com • $$$$

8 Bahía Salinas Beach Resort & Spa

The sunlight-filled rooms with bay views here are done up with elegant antique reproductions and contemporary furniture. There is a gourmet restaurant as well as a full-service spa. ◈ Map B5 • Carretera 301 Km 11, Cabo Rojo • 787 254 1213 • www.bahia salinas.com • $$$$

9 Hix Island House

The loft apartments in this zen-inspired hotel have bare concrete floors, hip furnishings, luxurious fabrics, and large windows that offer great views. There are private outdoor showers too. ◈ Map P5 • Carretera 995 Km 1.5, El Pilón, Vieques • 787 741 2302 • www.hix islandhouse.com • $$$$$

10 Inn on the Blue Horizon

The villas of this intimate hillside hotel exude romance and intentionally lack phones. The premises boast tennis courts, bicycles, and a renowned gourmet restaurant. ◈ Map P5 • Carretera 996 Km 4.2, Esperanza, Vieques • 787 741 0010 • www. innonthebluehorizon.com • $$$$

Left **Four Points by Sheraton Palmas del Mar Resort** Right **Copamarina Beach Resort**

TOP10 Beach Hotels

1 Villas del Mar Hau
With its colorful wooden cabins under shade trees and edging up to the beach, this low-key resort is one of the nicest places near Playa de Jobos. The rooms have attractive furnishings. Activities available here include tennis, volleyball, and kayaking. *Map C1 • Carretera 466 Km 8.9, Isabela • 787 872 2045 • hauhotelvillas.com • $$$*

2 Río Mar Beach Resort & Spa
This 672-room high-rise sprawls across a former coconut plantation near the beach. Its luxurious rooms are furnished in contemporary tropical-island fashion, with plush fabrics. Make the most of its superb watersports facilities, Oriental-themed spa, and 11 restaurants. *Map M2 • Bulevar Río Mar 6000, Río Grande • 787 888 6000 • www.wyndhamriomar.com • $$$$*

3 Four Points by Sheraton Palmas del Mar Resort
The rooms of this elegant beachfront hotel, tucked within the sprawling, gated Palmas del Mar community (see p97), have classical European styling, but lack ocean views. There are tennis courts, two golf courses, and children's facilities. *Map M4 • Candelero Dr 170, Humacao • 787 850 6000 • www.starwood-hotels.com • $$$$*

4 Embassy Suites Dorado del Mar
This all-suite resort, which is popular with families, towers over a large pool complex. Most rooms have ocean views and are furnished in a Caribbean style. Some are self-catering condos. There is a championship golf course here too. *Map J2 • Bulevar Dorado del Mar 201, Dorado • 787 796 6125 • embassysuites1.hilton.com • $$$*

5 El Conquistador Resort
The facilities at this vast resort, which occupies a stunning cliff-top perch, include a casino, water park, spa, championship golf course, and over 20 restaurants, bars, and lounges. The rooms and villas offer cosmopolitan decor. *Map N3 • Av Conquistador 1000, Fajardo • 787 863 1000 • www.elconresort.com • $$$$*

6 Copamarina Beach Resort
All the rooms at this hotel face a coral-tinged beach with canopied beds for lounging. Activities include parasailing and scuba diving. *Map D6 • Carretera 333 Km 6.5, Caña Gorda • 787 821 0505 • www.copamarina.com • $$$*

7 Caribe Playa Sea Beach Resort
This 1960s-era low-rise has a lovely shorefront setting, with hammocks slung between palms, and offers good value. Studio rooms vary – a "Mamey" room has a king-size bed. The restaurant offers romantic candlelit dinners alfresco. *Map L5 • Carretera 3 Km 112.1, Patillas • 787 839 6339 • www.caribeplaya.com • $$$*

8 W Retreat & Spa
A contemporary aesthetic meets luxurious Spanish-style villa-living at this retreat. Rooms are a blaze of whites, and French doors open to ocean views. There is a deluxe spa too. *Map P5 • Carretera 200 Km 3.2, Vieques • 787 741 4100 • www.whotels.com/explore • $$$$$*

9 Hotel Parador Palmas de Lucía
Nestled between beach and mountain, this motel-style hotel offers airy rooms with balconies that overlook a courtyard pool. This is a good spot for beach volleyball. *Map M5 • Carretera Panorámica 901, Yabucoa • 787 893 4423 • www.palmasdelucia.com • $$$*

10 Hilton Ponce Golf & Casino Resort
The ocean-view rooms here sport a lively tropical motif. Facilities include tennis courts, four restaurants, a casino, and a pool complex. *Map F5 • Av Caribe 1150, Ponce • 787 259 7676 • www.hiltoncaribbean.com • $$$*

Price Categories

For a standard, double room per night (with breakfast if included), taxes, and extra charges.

$	under $50
$$	$50–100
$$$	$100–150
$$$$	$150–250
$$$$$	over $250

Hacienda Gripiñas

TOP 10 Rural Hotels

1 Ceiba Country Inn
Surrounded by lush countryside, this mountainside bed-and-breakfast is a good option for bird-watchers. The El Yunque National Forest *(see pp14–15)* is a short drive away. The simply appointed but comfortable rooms have a tropical motif and offer ocean views. ◎ *Map N3 • Carretera 977 Km 1.2, Ceiba • 787 885 0471 • $$*

2 Hacienda Gripiñas
Historic charm pervades this 19th-century coffee estate in the shadow of Puerto Rico's highest peak. A rambling layout and wooden floors help add atmosphere to the simple rooms. This is a good base for hikes and horse-back riding. ◎ *Map F4 • Carretera 527 Km 2.5, Jayuya • 787 828 1/17 • www.hacienda gripinas.tripod.com • $$*

3 Parador Hacienda Juanita
This historic wooden plantation-turned-*parador* has a delightful mountain setting and continues to function as a coffee estate. The rooms are functional but cozy and include four-poster beds and ceiling fans. A rustic restaurant serves tasty meals on the premises and also has entertaining live folk music. ◎ *Map C4 • Carretera 105 Km 23.5, Maricao • 787 828 2550 • www.haciendajuanita.com • $$$*

4 Casa Grande Mountain Retreat
Once a coffee plantation, this bargain-priced mountain resort is wrapped in forest and boasts fabulous mountains vistas. Simply furnished cabins on stilts rise over a lush tropical garden, making for a beautiful setting. A colorful restaurant serves hearty meals. There are good hiking trails nearby. ◎ *Map E3 • Carretera 612 Km 0.4, Utuado • 787 894 3939 • www.hotelcasa grande.com • $$*

5 T.J. Ranch
Set on a coffee plantation amid dramatic limestone formations, this ranch has three comfortable cabins and makes a great base for hiking and bird-watching. It has a swimming pool, and serves meals in a thatched *bohío* (hut). ◎ *Map E3 • Carretera 146, Arecibo • 787 880 1217 • www.tjranch.com • $$$*

6 Parador Villas Sotomayor
Popular with Puerto Rican families, this countryside resort is surrounded by forested mountains and offers horseback riding, forest trails, and a swimming pool. Accommodations are in modern, well-equipped cabins. ◎ *Map E4 • Carretera 123 Km 36.7, Adjuntas • 787 829 1717 • www.paradorvillas sotomayor.com • $$$*

7 Casa Cubuy
A bird-watcher's delight, this simple mountain lodge on the south side of the El Yunque National Forest *(see pp14–15)* has sparsely furnished rooms that are airy and colorful and have balconies with good views. Breakfasts are included, and dinner is by reservation. ◎ *Map M3 • Carretera 191, Río Blanco • 787 874 6221 • www. casacubuy.com • $$*

8 Parador Baños de Coamo
This historic inn is known for its healing mineral pools. The ageing rooms are adequate, and the meals are satisfying and the leafy setting is peaceful. ◎ *Map H5 • Carretera 546 Km 1, Coamo • 787 825 2186 • $$*

9 Lago Vista Hotel
The 16 air-conditioned rooms overlooking Lake Guajataca have televisions, but the serenity and great hiking trails are the main lures here. There is also a swimming pool. ◎ *Map C3 • Carretera 119 Km 22.1, San Sebastián • 787 280 5522 • $$*

10 Parador El Buen Café Hotel
This is a modern hotel with stylish interiors, a pool, and an excellent restaurant and popular café. ◎ *Map D1 • Carretera 381 Km 84, Hatillo • 787 898 1000 • www.elbuen cafe.com • $$$*

General Index

Acknowledgments

The Author
Christopher P. Baker is an award-winning travel writer and photographer specializing in the Caribbean and Central America. His feature articles have appeared in more than 200 publications worldwide. His many books include the literary travelog *Mi Moto Fidel: Motorcycling Through Castro's Cuba*.

Photographer
Linda Whitwam

Maps
Martin Darlison, Encompass Graphics Ltd

Fact Checker
Hans-Ulrich Dillman, Textosdam

FOR DORLING KINDERSLEY

Publisher
Douglas Amrine

List Manager
Christine Stroyan

Design Manager
Sunita Gahir

Senior Editor
Sadie Smith

Project Editor
Alexandra Farrell

Art Editor
Nicola Erdpresser

Senior Cartographic Editor
Casper Morris

DTP Designer
Jason Little

Production Controller
Rebecca Short

Revisions Team
Carla Lopez de Azua, Neha Gupta, Claire Jones, Carly Madden, Alison McGill, Vikki Nousiainen, Khushboo Priya, Lucy Richards, Ellen Root, Sands Publishing Solutions, Susana Smith, Ajay Verma, Kelly Ann Voke

Picture Credits
Key: a-above; b-below/bottom; c-center; f-far; l-left; r-right; t-top.

The Publisher would like to thank the following individuals, companies and picture libraries for their kind permissions to reproduce their photographs:

4CORNERS IMAGES: SIME/ Gunter Grafenhain 1c.

ALAMY: Content Mine International 35tl; Chris A. Crumley 85tl; Mark Downey 7bl; Robert Fried 20cb, 22bc; Gastromedia 50tr; Nick Hanna 21tl; kpzfoto 52c; Y. Levy 50bl; John Maciiwinen 17tl; Donald Nausbaum 42tl; Nicholas Pitt 43cl; Redcarpetrpress 34br; Kevin Schafer 15cb; Visual & Written SL 54bl, 55cl.

THE BRIDGEMAN ART LIBRARY: © The Maas Gallery, London *Flaming June* c. 1895 oil on canvas Fredric Leighton 27tc.

CELSO A HERNANDEZ: 70tl.

CORBIS: Tony Aruzza 30bl; Atlantide Phototravel/Massimo Borchi 4-5; Bettmann 30t; Macduff Everton 26bc; Stephen Frink 19cr; Stephie Maze 42tr; Neal Preston 34tl; Charles E. Rotkin 42bl.

COLLECTION MUSEO DE ARTE DE PONCE. THE LUIS A. FERRÉ FOUNDATION INC., Ponce Puerto Rico: John Betancourt 26-27c, *The Glass Blowers* 1883 oil on panel (40.6 x 50.8 cm) Charles Frederick Ulrich 26cla; *Portrait of Claude Lorrain* 19th century Bronze (49.8 x 19.7 x 21.6 cm) Auguste Rodin 27cb; *Doubting Thomas* ca. 1620 oil on canvas (112.1 x 89.5 cm) Bernardo Strozzi 27cr.

OOF! RESTAURANTS & CATERING: 48tl.

PHOTOLIBRARY: Creatas Creatas 18-19c; Reinhard Dirscherl 76tr; Du Boisberranger Jean 40-41; J Kevin Foltz 100-101; Kim Karpeles 56-57; Ken Welsh 12-13c, 80-81.

Photos of PUERTO RICO.COM: 21bc, 75bl.

EL SAN JUAN RESORT & CASINO: 64tl, 114tr.

VISAGE MEDIA SERVICES: Getty Images 31tl; Erich Auerbach/Stringer Collection 34tr.

Pull-Out Map – All images © DK Images and Rough Guides.

All other images are © Dorling Kindersley. For further information see www.dkimages.com

---

Special Editions of DK Travel Guides

Phrase Book

In an Emergency

Help!	**¡Socorro**	soh-**koh**-roh
Stop!	**¡Pare!**	**pah**-reh
Call a doctor!	**¡Llame a un médico!**	**yah**-meh ah **oon meh**-dee-koh
Call an ambulance!	**¡Llame a una ambulancia!**	**yah**-meh ah **oonah** ahm-boo-**lahn**-thee-ah
Call the police!	**¡Llame a la policía!**	**yah**-meh ah lah poh-lee-**thee**-ah
Call the fire department!	**¡Llame a los bomberos!**	**yah**-meh ah lohs bohm-**beh**-rohs
Where is the nearest telephone?	**¿Dónde está el teléfono más próximo?**	**dohn**-deh ehs-**tah** ehl teh-**leh**-foh-noh **mahs prohx**-ee-moh
Where is the nearest hospital?	**¿Dónde está el hospital más próximo?**	**dohn**-deh ehs-**tah** ehl ohs-pee-**tahl mahs prohx**-ee-moh

Communication Essentials

Yes	**Sí**	see
No	**No**	noh
Please	**Por favor**	pohr fah-**vohr**
Thank you	**Gracias**	**grah**-thee-ahs
Excuse me	**Perdone**	pehr-**doh**-neh
Hello	**Hola**	**oh**-lah
Goodbye	**Adiós**	ah-dee-**ohs**
Goodnight	**Buenas noches**	**bweh**-nahs **noh**chehs
Morning	**La mañana**	lah mah-**nyah**-nah
Afternoon	**La tarde**	lah **tahr**-deh
Evening	**La tarde**	lah **tahr**-deh
Yesterday	**Ayer**	ah-**yehr**
Today	**Hoy**	oy
Tomorrow	**Mañana**	mah-**nya**-nah
Here	**Aquí**	ah-**kee**
There	**Allí**	ah-**yee**
What?	**¿Qué?**	keh
When?	**¿Cuándo?**	**kwahn**-doh
Why?	**¿Por qué?**	pohr-**keh**
Where?	**¿Dónde?**	**dohn**-deh

Useful Phrases

How are you?	**¿Cómo está usted?**	**koh**-moh ehs-**tah** oos-**tehd**
Very well, thank you	**Muy bien, gracias**	mwee bee-**ehn grah**-thee-ahs
Pleased to meet you	**Encantado de conocerle**	ehn-kahn-**tah**-doh deh koh-noh-**thehr**-leh
See you soon	**Hasta pronto.**	ahs-tah **prohn**-toh
Where is/are ...?	**¿Dónde está/están ...?**	**dohn**-deh ehs-**tah**/ehs-**tahn**
How far is it to ...?	**¿Cuántos metros/ kilómetros hay de aquí a ...?**	**kwahn**-tohs **meh**-trohs/kee-**loh**-meh-trohs **eye** deh ah-**kee** ah
Which way to ...?	**¿Por dónde se va a ...?**	pohr **dohn**-deh seh **bah** ah
Do you speak English?	**¿Habla inglés?**	**ah**-blah een-**glehs**
I don't understand	**No comprendo**	noh kohm-**prehn**-doh
I'm sorry	**Lo siento**	loh see-**ehn**-toh

Useful Words

big	**grande**	**grahn**-deh
small	**pequeño**	peh-**keh**-nyoh
hot	**caliente**	kah-lee-**ehn**-the
enough	**bastante**	bahs-**tahn**-the
open	**abierto**	ah-bee-**ehr**-toh
closed	**cerrado**	thehr-**rah**-doh
left	**izquierda**	eeth-key-**ehr**-dah
right	**derecha**	deh-**reh**-chah
near	**cerca**	**thehr**-kah
far	**lejos**	**leh**-hohs
up	**arriba**	ah-**ree**-bah
down	**abajo**	ah-**bah**-hoh
cold	**frío**	**free**-oh
good	**bueno**	**bweh**-noh
bad	**malo**	**mah**-loh
early	**temprano**	tehm-**prah**-noh
late	**tarde**	**tahr**-deh
toilet	**lavabos, servicios**	lah-**vah**-bohs seh-**bee**-thee-ohs

Shopping

How much does this cost?	**¿Cuánto cuesta esto?**	**kwahn**-toh **kwehs**-tah ehs-toh
Do you have?	**¿Tienen?**	tee-**yeh**-nehn
expensive	**caro**	**kahr**-oh
cheap	**barato**	bah-**rah**-toh

Sightseeing

art gallery	**el museo de arte**	ehl moo-**seh**-oh deh **ahr**-the
cathedral	**la catedral**	lah kah-teh-**drahl**
church	**la iglesia**	lah ee-**gleh**-see-ah
	la basílica	lah bah-**see**-lee-kah
garden	**el jardín**	ehl hahr-**deen**
library	**la biblioteca**	lah bee-blee-oh-**teh**-kah
museum	**el museo**	ehl moo-**seh**-oh
tourist information office	**la oficina de turismo**	lah oh-fee-**thee**-nah deh too-**rees**-moh
town hall	**el ayuntamiento**	ehl ah-yoon-tah-mee-**ehn**-toh
closed for holiday	**cerrado por vacaciones**	thehr-**rah**-doh pohr bah-kah-thee-**oh**-nehs
bus station	**la estación de autobuses**	lah ehs-tah-ee-**ohn** deh owtoh-**boo**-sehs
railway station	**la estación de trenes**	lah ehs-tah-thee-**ohn** deh **treh**-nehs

Staying in a Hotel

Do you have a vacant room?	**¿Tienen una habitación libre?**	tee-**eh**-nehn oo-nah ah-bee-tah-thee-**ohn** lee-breh
double room	**habitación doble**	ah-bee-tah-thee-**ohn** doh-bleh
with double bed	**con cama de matrimonio**	kohn **kah**-mah deh mah-tree-**moh**-nee-oh
key	**la llave**	lah **yah**-veh

Note: In Puerto Rican Spanish, the soft "c" sound is pronounced as an "s" instead of the lisped "th" of Castilian Spanish.

Eating Out

The bill	**La cuenta**	lah **kwehn**-tah
please	**por favor**	pohr fah-**vohr**
I am a	**Soy**	soy beh-heh-tah-
vegetarian	**vegetariano/a**	ree-**ah**-no/na
waitress/	**camarera/**	kah-mah-**reh**-rah
waiter	**camarero**	kah-mah-**reh**-roh
menu	**la carta**	lah **kahr**-tah
fixed-price	**menú del**	meh-**noo** dehl
menu	**día**	**dee**-ah
wine list	**la carta de**	lah **kahr**-tah deh
	vinos	**bee**-nohs
knife	**un cuchillo**	oon koo-**chee**-yoh
fork	**un tenedor**	oon teh-nch **dohr**
spoon	**una cuchara**	oo-nah koo-**chah**-rah
breakfast	**el desayuno**	ehl deh-sah-**yoo**-noh
lunch	**la comida/**	lah koh-**mee**-dah/
	el almuerzo	ehl ahl-**mwehr**-thoh
dinner	**la cena**	lah **theh**-nah
main course	**el segundo**	ehl pree-**mehr**
	plato	**plah**-toh
coffee	**el café**	ehl kah-**feh**
rare	**poco hecho**	poh-koh **eh**-choh
medium	**medio hecho**	**meh**-dee-oh **eh**-choh
well done	**muy hecho**	mwee **eh**-choh

Menu Decoder

al horno	ahl **ohr**-noh	baked
asado	ah-**sah**-doh	roast
el aceite	ah-**thee-eh**-teh	oil
las aceitunas	ah-theh-**toon**-ahs	olives
el agua mineral	**ah**-gwa mee-neh-**rahl**	mineral water
sin gas/con gas	seen gas/ kohn gas	still/ sparkling
el ajo	**ah**-hoh	garlic
el arroz	ahr-**rohth**	rice
el azúcar	ah-**thoo**-kahr	sugar
la carne	**kahr**-neh	meat
la cebolla	theh-**boh**-yah	onion
la cerveza	thehr-**beh**-thah	beer
el cerdo	**therh**-doh	pork
el chocolate	choh-koh-**lah**-teh	chocolate
el chorizo	choh-**ree**-thoh	red sausage
el cordero	kohr-**deh**-roh	lamb
el fiambre	fee-**ahm**-breh	cold meat
frito	**free**-toh	fried
la fruta	**froo**-tah	fruit
los frutos secos	**froo**-tohs **seh**-kohs	nuts
las gambas	**gahm**-bahs	prawns
el helado	eh-**lah**-doh	ice cream
el huevo	oo-**eh**-voh	egg
el jamón serrano	hah-**mohn** sehr-**rah**-noh	cured ham
el jerez	heh-**rehz**	sherry
la langosta	lahn-**gohs**-tah	lobster
la leche	**leh**-cheh	milk
el limón	lee-**mohn**	lemon
la limonada	lee-moh-**nah**-dah	lemonade
la mantequilla	mahn-teh-**kee**-yah	butter
la manzana	mahn-**thah**-nah	apple
los mariscos	mah-**rees**-kohs	seafood
la menestra	meh-**nehs**-trah	vegetable stew
la naranja	nah-**rahn**-hah	orange
el pan	**pahn**	bread
el pastel	pahs-**tehl**	cake
las patatas	pah-**tah**-tahs	potatoes
el pescado	pehs-**kah**-doh	fish
la pimienta	pee-mee-**yehn**-tah	pepper
el plátano	**plah**-tah-noh	banana
el pollo	**poh**-yoh	chicken
el postre	**pohs**-treh	dessert
el queso	**keh**-soh	cheese
la sal	sahl	salt
las salchichas	sahl-**chee**-chahs	sausages
la salsa	**sahl**-sah	sauce
seco	**seh**-koh	dry
el solomillo	soh-loh-**mee**-yoh	sirloin
la sopa	**soh**-pah	soup
la tarta	**tahr**-tah	pie/cake
el té	teh	tea
la ternera	tehr-**neh**-rah	beef
las tostadas	tohs-**tah**-dahs	toast
el vinagre	bee-**nah**-greh	vinegar
el vino blanco	**bee**-noh **blahn**-koh	white wine
el vino rosado	**bee**-noh roh-**sah**-doh	rosé wine
el vino tinto	**bee**-noh **teen**-toh	red wine

Numbers

0	**cero**	**theh**-roh
1	**uno**	**oo**-noh
2	**dos**	dohs
3	**tres**	trehs
4	**cuatro**	**kwa**-troh
5	**cinco**	**theen**-koh
6	**seis**	says
7	**siete**	**see**-eh-the
8	**ocho**	**oh**-choh
9	**nueve**	**nweh**-veh
10	**diez**	dee-**ehth**
11	**once**	**ohn**-theh
12	**doce**	**doh**-theh
20	**veinte**	**beh**-een-the
21	**veintiuno**	beh-een-tee-**oo**-noh
22	**veintidós**	beh-een-tee-**dohs**
30	**treinta**	**treh**-een-tah
40	**cuarenta**	kwah-**rehn**-tah
100	**cien**	thee-**ehn**
101	**ciento uno**	thee-**ehn**-toh oo-noh
200	**doscientos**	dohs-thee-**ehn**-tohs

Time

one minute	**un minuto**	oon mee-**noo**-toh
one hour	**una hora**	**oo**-na **oh**-rah
half an hour	**media hora**	**meh**-dee-a **oh**-rah
Monday	**lunes**	**loo**-nehs
Tuesday	**martes**	**mahr**-tehs
Wednesday	**miércoles**	mee-**ehr**-koh-lehs
Thursday	**jueves**	hoo-**weh**-vehs
Friday	**viernes**	bee-**ehr**-nehs
Saturday	**sábado**	**sah**-bah-doh
Sunday	**domingo**	doh-**meen**-goh

Note: In Puerto Rican the "s" and "d" at the end of words is often not pronounced. So, muchas gracias (thank you) is "mucha gracia".

Puerto Rico: Selected Town Index

San Juan: Selected Street Index